Poverty

Editor: Tracy Biram

Volume 377

independence
educational publishers

First published by Independence Educational Publishers

The Studio, High Green

Great Shelford

Cambridge CB22 5EG

England

© Independence 2020

Copyright

Photocopy licence

ISBN-13: 978 1 86168 834 7

Printed in Great Britain

Zenith Print Group

Contents

Introduction

Poverty is Volume 377 in the **issues** series. The aim of the series is to offer current, diverse information about important issues in our world, from a UK perspective.

ABOUT POVERTY

Approximately 14 million people in the UK – a fifth of the population – live in poverty. Food bank use and homelessness have both seen a huge increase in recent years. This book explores poverty in the UK and around the globe. It looks at the causes and consequences of poverty and the impact on families and communities. It also considers some of the efforts being made to eradicate poverty, once and for all.

OUR SOURCES

Titles in the **issues** series are designed to function as educational resource books, providing a balanced overview of a specific subject.

The information in our books is comprised of facts, articles and opinions from many different sources, including:

♦ Newspaper reports and opinion pieces

♦ Website factsheets

♦ Magazine and journal articles

♦ Statistics and surveys

♦ Government reports

♦ Literature from special interest groups.

A NOTE ON CRITICAL EVALUATION

Because the information reprinted here is from a number of different sources, readers should bear in mind the origin of the text and whether the source is likely to have a particular bias when presenting information (or when conducting their research). It is hoped that, as you read about the many aspects of the issues explored in this book, you will critically evaluate the information presented.

It is important that you decide whether you are being presented with facts or opinions. Does the writer give a biased or unbiased report? If an opinion is being expressed, do you agree with the writer? Is there potential bias to the 'facts' or statistics behind an article?

ASSIGNMENTS

In the back of this book, you will find a selection of assignments designed to help you engage with the articles you have been reading and to explore your own opinions. Some tasks will take longer than others and there is a mixture of design, writing and research-based activities that you can complete alone or in a group.

FURTHER RESEARCH

At the end of each article we have listed its source and a website that you can visit if you would like to conduct your own research. Please remember to critically evaluate any sources that you consult and consider whether the information you are viewing is accurate and unbiased.

Useful Websites

www.bigissue.com

www.borgenproject.org

www.fee.org

www.focus-economics.com

www.ifs.org.uk

www.independent.co.uk

www.jrf.org.uk

www.manchestereveningnews.co.uk

www.news-decoder.com

www.poverty.ac.uk

www.publicfinance.co.uk

www.telegraph.co.uk

www.theconversation.com

www.theguardian.com

www.thisismoney.co.uk

www.trusselltrust.org

www.unherd.com

www.unicef.org

views-voices.oxfam.org.uk

www.weforum.org

What is poverty?

Poverty is when your resources are well below your minimum needs.

How does JRF (Joseph Rowntree Foundation) define poverty in the UK?

Poverty affects millions of people in the UK. Poverty means not being able to heat your home, pay your rent or buy the essentials for your children. It means waking up every day facing insecurity, uncertainty and impossible decisions about money. It means facing marginalisation – and even discrimination – because of your financial circumstances. The constant stress it causes can lead to problems that deprive people of the chance to play a full part in society.

How is poverty measured in the UK?

There is no single best measure of poverty. It is a complex problem that needs a range of measures telling us different things.

JRF launched a comprehensive strategy to Solve Poverty for all ages and places in the UK. We have set out a long-term and wide-ranging approach that looks beyond temporary political change, aiming for a major shift in attitudes, society and the economy.

Measures include:

♦ JRF's Minimum Income Standard (MIS) – MIS itself is not a measure of poverty, but is what the public has told us is sufficient income to afford a minimum acceptable standard of living

♦ relative income poverty, where households have less than 60% of contemporary median income

♦ absolute income poverty, where households have less than 60% of the median income in 2010/11, uprated by inflation

♦ material deprivation, where you can't afford certain essential items and activities

♦ destitution, where you can't afford basics such as shelter, heating and clothing.

Relative and absolute poverty can be presented before and after housing costs (these include rent or mortgage interest, buildings insurance and water rates) and are presented after direct taxes and National Insurance, including Council Tax.

Levels of poverty

There are 3 levels of poverty

Income at minimum income standard or better: able to afford a decent standard of living

Income below minimum income standard: getting by day-to-day under pressure, difficult to manage unexpected costs and events

Not enough income: falling substantially short of a decent standard of living, high chance of not meeting needs

Destitute: can't afford to eat, keep clean and stay warm and dry

MIS
(Minimum income standard)

75% MIS

Destitution

What causes poverty in the UK?

The causes of poverty are things that reduce your resources or increase your needs and the costs of meeting them. Some of these causes can also be consequences, creating a cycle that traps you. Life events and moments of transition – getting sick, bereavement, redundancy or relationship breakdown – are common triggers for poverty.

Some of the causes of poverty in the UK today are:

♦ **unemployment and low-paid jobs lacking prospects and security (or a lack of jobs):** too many jobs do not provide decent pay, prospects or security. Many places have concentrations of these jobs or do not have enough jobs. Low pay and unemployment can also lead to inadequate savings or pensions.

♦ **low levels of skills or education:** young people and adults without the necessary skills and qualifications can find it difficult to get a job, especially one with security, prospects and decent pay.

♦ **an ineffective benefit system:** the level of welfare benefits for some people – either in work, seeking work or unable to work because of health or care issues – is not enough to avoid poverty, when combined with other resources and high costs. The benefit system is often confusing and hard to engage with, causing errors and delays. The system can also make it risky and difficult for some to move into jobs or increase their working hours. Low take-up of some benefits also increases poverty.

♦ **high costs:** the high cost of housing and essential goods and services (e.g. credit, gas, electricity, water, Council Tax, telephone or broadband) creates poverty. Some groups face particularly high costs related to where they live, increased needs (for example, personal care for

disabled people) or because they are paying a 'poverty premium' – where people in poverty pay more for the same goods and services.

♦ **discrimination:** discrimination against people because of their class, gender, ethnicity, disability, age, sexuality, religion or parental status (or even poverty itself) can prevent people from escaping poverty through good qualifications or jobs, and can restrict access to services.

♦ **weak relationships:** a child who does not receive warm and supportive parenting can be at higher risk of poverty in later life, because of the impact on their development, education and social and emotional skills. Family relationships breaking down can also lead to poverty.

♦ **abuse, trauma or chaotic lives:** for small numbers of people, problematic or chaotic use of drugs and alcohol can deepen and prolong poverty. Neglect or abuse as a child or trauma in adult life can also cause poverty, as the impact on mental health can lead to unemployment, low earnings and links to homelessness and substance misuse. Being in prison and having a criminal record can also deepen poverty, by making it harder to get a job and weakening relationships.

Consequences of poverty in the UK

Some of the consequences of poverty are:

♦ health problems

♦ housing problems

♦ being a victim or perpetrator of crime

♦ drug or alcohol problems

♦ lower educational achievement

♦ poverty itself – poverty in childhood increases the risk of unemployment and low pay in adulthood, and lower savings in later life

♦ homelessness

♦ teenage parenthood

♦ relationship and family problems

♦ biological effects – poverty early in a child's life can have a harmful effect on their brain development

How to solve poverty in the UK

Solving poverty is not quick or easy, but it is possible, starting with a vision, commitment and a plan.

We need a concerted effort by all – employers and businesses, private and social landlords, local and national policy-makers, the media, and all citizens and communities, including people in poverty themselves – if we want the UK to be free from poverty.

July 2020

The above information is reprinted with kind permission from JRF.
©Joseph Rowntree Foundation 2020

www.jrf.org.uk

Living standards, poverty and inequality in the UK: 2020

Report by Pascale Bourquin, Robert Joyce and Agnes Norris Keiller

This report examines how living standards – most commonly measured by households' incomes – were changing in the UK up to approximately the eve of the current COVID-19 crisis, using the latest official household income data covering years up to 2018–19. We particularly focus on how this differed for different groups, and what this meant for poverty and inequality. It gives us a comprehensive account of where we stood before the current crisis, including for groups who we now know have subsequently had their economic lives turned upside down.

Key findings:

♦ **The COVID-19 crisis hit at a time when income growth had already been extremely disappointing for some years. Median (middle) household income was essentially the same in 2018–19 (the latest data) as in 2015–16.** This stalling itself came after only a short-lived recovery from the Great Recession. The combined effect had been a decade of unprecedented poor improvements in living standards, with average income before housing costs having grown less than over any other 10-year period since records began in 1961.

♦ **The main culprit for the latest choking-off of real income growth had been a rise in inflation from 2016.** This was partly due to the depreciation of sterling following the Brexit referendum.

♦ **For people aged 60 or over, median income was 12% higher in 2018–19 than before the previous recession in 2007–08, while among the rest of the population it was only 3% higher.** However, in recent years, income growth had stalled for old and young alike.

♦ **Trends among low-income households had been worse still – they had experienced five years of real income stagnation between 2013–14 and 2018–19.** This was entirely due to falls in income from working-age benefits and tax credits, which offset growth in employment incomes. Working-age benefits were frozen in cash terms, so the rise in inflation from 2016 reduced their value in real terms by 5%.

♦ **Overall relative poverty (using incomes measured after housing costs are deducted (AHC) was 22% in 2018–19, and it has fluctuated little since the early 2000s. For particular groups, though, we have seen more change**. Relative poverty among working-age adults without children has fallen since 2011–12, while relative child poverty has increased by 3 percentage points – the most sustained rise in relative child poverty since the early 1990s.

♦ **Absolute AHC poverty was 20% in 2018–19 – virtually unchanged over the last two years.** The recent lack of progress in reducing absolute poverty is disappointing: it only fell by 1.4 percentage points between 2010–11 and 2018–19 whereas reductions over an equivalent period in previous decades were around 5–6 percentage points on average.

♦ **Workers whose livelihoods look most at risk during the COVID-19 crisis already tended to have relatively low incomes, and were relatively likely to be in poverty, prior to the onset of the crisis.** Employees working in 'shut-down sectors', such as hospitality, were already almost twice as likely to be in poverty as other employees, and poverty rates were higher still for self-employed people working in these sectors. Cleaners and hairdressers stand out as groups with higher poverty rates than other workers who are unlikely to be able to work from home.

♦ **In 2018–19, only 12% of non-pensioners lived in households with no one in paid work, down by a third from 18% in 1994–95.** This progress is highly likely to be undermined by the COVID-19 pandemic.

♦ **Despite temporary increases in benefits announced in response to the pandemic, the benefits system in 2020 provides less support to out-of-work households than in 2011.** Average benefit entitlement among workless households is 10% lower in 2020–21 than it would have been without any policy changes since 2011, and among workless households with children it is 12% lower. These cuts in generosity are mainly due to the 'benefits freeze' and the introduction of universal credit; without the temporary increases, they would have been 15% and 16% respectively.

25 June 2020

End of year stats – The Trussell Trust

Record 1.9m food bank parcels given to people in the past year as the Trussell Trust calls for governments at all levels to use their powers to make sure everyone can afford the essentials.

Between 1 April 2019 and 31 March 2020, the Trussell Trust's food bank network distributed 1.9 million three-day emergency food supplies to people in crisis, an 18% increase on the previous year. More than seven hundred thousand of these went to children.

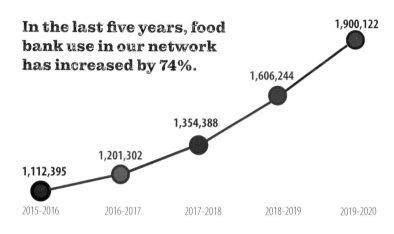

In the last five years, food bank use in our network has increased by 74%.

1,112,395 — 2015-2016
1,201,302 — 2016-2017
1,354,388 — 2017-2018
1,606,244 — 2018-2019
1,900,122 — 2019-2020

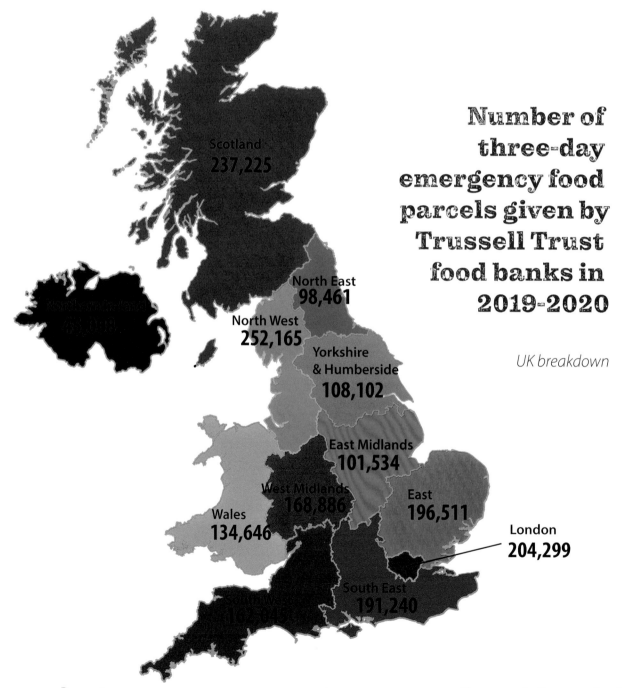

Number of three-day emergency food parcels given by Trussell Trust food banks in 2019-2020

UK breakdown

Scotland **237,225**

North East **98,461**

North West **252,165**

Yorkshire & Humberside **108,102**

East Midlands **101,534**

West Midlands **168,886**

East **196,511**

Wales **134,646**

London **204,299**

South East **191,240**

"This year has been an extraordinarily difficult one, with many more people across the country facing destitution as a result of the coronavirus pandemic. Food banks carry on, working as tirelessly as ever, to support people in crisis through the unprecedented challenge the pandemic continues to pose. The statistics in our 2019/2020 report show the situation in food banks up until the end of March, before the true economic impact of the pandemic had hit.

Despite this, we see a rise in the number of people being forced to use a food bank yet again.

This constant rise in food bank use, year after year, cannot continue. More and more people are struggling to eat because they simply cannot afford food – and when we look to the year ahead, it's likely even more people will be forced into destitution. This is not right."

"We know this situation can be turned around – that's why we're campaigning to create a future where no one needs a food bank. Our benefits system is supposed to protect us all from being swept into poverty and while additional government measures have helped some people stay afloat this year, clearly more needs to be done. That's why we united with partners from across the charity sector in urging the UK government to make sure everyone can afford the essentials through the economic downturn. And we want to see governments at all levels doing everything in their power to protect people from financial hardship."

"We have outlined what needs to be done – it's in our power to protect one another, we've seen it during this health crisis, and we need it to continue during this economic one."

Emma Revie

Chief Executive

Primary reasons for referral to Trussell Trust food banks in 2019-20

The top three reasons for referral to a food bank in the Trussell Trust network in 2019–20 were low income, benefit delays and benefit changes.

39%

LOW INCOME

17%

BENEFIT DELAYS

15%

BENEFIT CHANGES

Governments at all levels need to use their powers to support people

Our statistics for 2019/20 show that food banks were already experiencing record levels of need before the coronavirus pandemic struck. We have seen significant increases since the economic fallout of the crisis. This continued increase in food bank use cannot continue.

That's why we are coming together with partners from across the charity sector to urge governments at all levels to use their powers to make sure that everyone can afford the essentials through the economic downturn and beyond.

We have previously outlined what governments need to do – it is within our power to make sure we protect one another during this crisis.

Food bank statistics for previous financial years with regional breakdown

	2013/14	2014/15	2015/16	2016/17	2017/18	2018/19	2019/20
UK	913,982	1,091,282	1,112,395	1,201,302	1,354,388	1,606,244	1,900,122
England	749,667	866,481	86,3870	920,170	1,046,807	1,235,892	1,483,243
Scotland	72,487	119,212	135,943	150,095	173,526	217,006	237,225
Wales	79,996	87,995	86,314	97,144	100,362	116,087	134,646
N.Ireland	11,832	17,654	26,268	33,893	33,693	37,259	45,008
North East	59,634	88,248	76,523	62,280	65,218	89,479	98,461
North West	138,005	158,079	160,803	175,645	198,830	225,188	252,165
Yorkshire & Humberside	36,867	58,939	66,303	70,307	79,502	90,245	108,102
West Midlands	94,024	104,374	103,702	111,760	121,039	142,900	168,886
East Midlands	40,380	45,484	49,366	56,791	67,078	78,229	101,534
East	88,703	102,319	103,668	116,356	130,493	157,243	196,511
London	99,925	108,373	112,124	113,701	137,923	169,734	204,299
South West	99,536	100,188	93,701	104,095	121,826	133,287	162,045
South East	92,593	100,477	97,680	109,235	124,898	149,587	191,240

What do these stats show?

Our statistics are a measure of volume rather than unique users, and on average people needed around two food bank referrals in the last year. The data is collected using an online system into which food banks enter data from each food bank voucher, and the number of three-day emergency food supplies is recorded.

For example, if a family of three was referred to a food bank twice in one year, this would count as six supplies on the system because it would reflect six instances on which a supply went to someone in the household. However, if a family of three were only referred to a food bank once, this would count as three supplies.

Trussell Trust figures cannot be used to fully explain the scale of food bank use across the UK, because our figures relate to food banks in our network and not to the hundreds of independent food aid providers. There are more than 1,200 food bank centres in our network across the UK. Research from the Independent Food Aid Network suggests these centres account for roughly two-thirds of all emergency food bank provision in the UK.

Benefit payments at historic low

A decade of austerity, the freezing of benefit levels and the introduction of universal credit have helped take benefit payments to their lowest level since 1948, finds a new report from the IPPR (Institute for Public Policy Research), 'Social (in)security: reforming the UK's safety net'.

The welfare reforms of 2015 (the benefit cap, two-child limit and benefits freeze) combined with some of the most severe cuts the welfare system has seen, has resulted in poverty now growing again, particularly among pensioners, children and those in work.

It asks whether the system can be effective when funding is at an all-time low:

"When Unemployment Benefit was first introduced in 1948 it was equivalent to 20 per cent of average weekly earnings, whereas comparable Universal Credit Standard Allowance payments have fallen to just 12.5 per cent of average earnings today."

The report finds that the system is at breaking point with some claimants in a constant state of financial insecurity. Clare McNeil, IPPR Associate Director and lead author of the report, said:

"It is remarkable that in post-war Britain the support for those living in poverty was closer to average earnings than it is today. This is the very simple fact that lies behind the record levels of personal debt, rising use of food banks and increasing destitution that we see in the UK."

The report also argues that the claims that restricting social security payments to subsistence levels or below, combined with strong sanctions, provide a strong incentive to work do not match the evidence. The report finds that, by contrast, "people need a degree of financial security in order to be able to make choices and provide for their family in order to secure and maintain work."

Ahead of the election, the think tank is calling on political parties to end the 'security deficit' by investing £8.4 billion emergency funding package into the benefit system every year over the next parliament. It also calls for a fundamental re-engineering of Universal Credit, including capping debt reduction payments, reducing waiting times for payment and the severity of sanctions, increasing work allowances and reducing the taper rate to 60%. This programme would be far more effective at raising the incomes of households in the bottom half of the income distribution than raising the National Insurance threshold. It notes that: "While the Conservative government has held steadfast to its flagship policy, the Labour party has now committed to 'scrapping universal credit', while the Liberal Democrats have said they will fix the problems with UC and 'construct a new benefits system' which provides dignity and respect. The SNP have also said the system should be 'radically reformed'."

Is the situation even worse than the IPPR suggests?

The seminal analysis by Nobel Prize winning economist Richard Stone (1997) showed that in 1688 the average income of pauper families was 16% of average income.

Therefore, Universal Credit Allowance payments are today - at 12.5% of average earnings - not only less generous, compared with average incomes, than at any time since the beginning of the Welfare State in 1948; they also appear to be relatively less generous than the 1599-1601 Old Poor Law system established during the reign of Elizabeth 1st.

Nov 25 2019

For full details see: 'Social (in)security:Reforming the UK's social safety net' by Clare McNeil, Dean Hochlaf and Harry Quilter-Pinner, IPPR, November 2019.

Available at:

https://www.ippr.org/research/publications/social-insecurity.

The ticking time bomb of lockdown poverty is about to explode

By Alexandra Phillips

One of the most moving stories from lockdown is that of the Assistant Headteacher in Grimsby who walked 5 miles every day, lugging a heavy rucksack packed with books and sandwiches to ensure that the most vulnerable children in his school weren't just up to date with work, but wouldn't go hungry. In his school, four out of ten of the 300 pupils live in deprivation.

I would imagine for most *Telegraph* subscribers, this sort of poverty here in the UK, where children are not even guaranteed food, is an alien concept. Not for Marcus Rashford, who himself grew up knowing hunger pains and watched while his mother toiled seemingly endless hours and still struggled to make ends meet.

The footballer raised £20 million to provide food parcels for 3 million children during lockdown and has petitioned the Government to provide free school lunches over the summer break. The response has been a curt dismissal of the proposed scheme and a tastelessly lofty response on Twitter from the Work and Pensions Secretary who saw fit to high-handedly dismiss his assertion that families might see water supplies disconnected while ignoring every other Tweet addressing the financial black hole faced by countless families up and down the country.

Currently 1.3 million students are entitled to free school meals, with an estimated 200,000 unlikely to eat today. This is not about affording a new pair of trainers, nor even having computing equipment to stay up to date with online lessons during lockdown, with one quarter of pupils unable to log on for this reason and a third failing to keep up with schoolwork. This is about the very basics of living – access to nutritious sustenance.

Poverty is something that many of us either do not realise, or do not want to realise, exists in our country. It is a painful and shameful admission of our nation's failings. But it is indubitably far more painful and shameful for those caught in the maelstrom.

It could soon become the narrative of the next decade unless the Government wakes up to the mounting disaster facing those already on the margins.

With more than 600,000 people unemployed during lockdown and the number of people claiming work-related benefits increasing by 23 per cent to 2.8 million, it is not those in Government, nor the civil service, who will soon be facing the need to go to food banks.

It will be the most vulnerable often engaged in the casual economy, who suffer from a lockdown policy that saw many middle classes furloughed on taxpayer cash, or those who could work from home perhaps enjoying the extra time spent with family and merrily skip the commute, while those already living hand-to-mouth were left without a formalised safety net. Now, half of those on £10 an hour are projected to face unemployment, catapulting families already struggling to provide the necessities into hopelessness and extreme vulnerability.

Poverty in the UK will not only become the chronic side effect of Covid-19. For a great many, it has also been the determining factor. People in deprived communities have been twice as likely to die from the disease than their more affluent counterparts.

Metabolic syndrome connected to obesity, heart disease and diabetes has been a death sentence for the majority of Covid-19 fatalities.

Contrary to common sense while talking about poverty-related hunger, we also find the flipside of poverty is obesity. Many parents up and down the country, unable to afford a three pack of avocados from Waitrose or a punnet of English strawberries, even when on special offer, reach for high in sugar and fat ultra-processed cupboard foods that often come at a bargain price tag and can be prepared and consumed by a minor while the parent goes out to work.

The ticking time bomb of lockdown-related poverty is about to explode and for those of us, like me, who grew up in a household of hand-me-downs, it will all-too-predictably impact those with fewer opportunities who can feel as though they exist under a cloak of invisibility.

The Government needs to embark upon drastic measures to get the blue collar demographic mobilised and working, opening pubs and bars, releasing all fit and healthy adults to re-engage fully with the economy. Right now it is displaying an almost myopic focus on grey and white collar unionised professions with one eye on the headlines. Unless something changes soon, we will see hundreds of thousands of children's lives laid to waste at the altar of public perception and polling.

6 June 2020

How sudden changes can leave us struggling to hold back the tide of poverty

Unexpected events can completely change the course of our lives, plunging us into hardship and eroding the stability and security we all need. Paul Brook spoke to two people who have gone from running businesses to bringing up their children on their own on a low income.

By Paul Brook

As JRF's new UK Poverty 2019/20 report shows, too many people in our society today are struggling to get by, leading insecure and precarious lives, and held back from improving their living standards. Something like losing your job or a relationship breakdown can be enough to sweep you into troubled waters.

When we spoke to parents on low incomes about housing, work and social security as part of the UK Poverty project, many of their comments reflected a sense of insecurity: "no stability", "a constant struggle", "no financial control", "can't plan for anything".

Moses Zikusoka, 54, and Elizabeth Cullen, 56, know what it's like to be hit by a sudden change in circumstances.

"It's been really tough"

Moses grew up in the UK after his family left Uganda in the 1970s. He got his MBA in Marketing before going on to work for Coca-Cola in Europe and Africa, then became Managing Director of QG Saatchi and Saatchi in Kampala, Uganda, before founding and developing his own events services business there.

After the breakdown of a relationship, he returned to London as a single father, wanting to give his three boys the same opportunities he'd had.

"I came back in 2016 to a very changed Britain," he says. "Despite my experience and knowledge, I had to start all over again, as a single parent.

"When I came back to the UK it was quite demoralising. I underestimated how hard it would be to start again. It's been really tough financially. I'd never claimed benefits before. I was used to working in a senior role, and I'm now earning half of what I earned 15 years ago, but I have to accept the circumstances. Being a single parent is not the end of the world. I have done many things in my life and I'm a very positive person. The benefits are a stop-gap."

"The worst time of my life"

Elizabeth has been raising her two sons on her own since her partner left in 2003, and lives in a houseboat that he owns.

"I'm in a difficult situation," she says. "I didn't marry their father. He's a wealthy man. In 2008 he got a court order that I could only live in one of his houses while one of the children was in full-time education, He's now trying to get us out of the house. I'm struggling with the law for equal rights for cohabitees."

In 2018, Elizabeth co-wrote an article with Sir Vince Cable, former leader of the Liberal Democrats and Elizabeth's former constituency MP, about the law on cohabiting relationships. This excerpt explains the problems she faces:

"When relationships break down, common decency and common sense often prevail and separation, while painful, is amicable or at least civil. But there are some cases where cruelty, vindictiveness, revenge or indifference play a large part and one partner (usually, but not always, the woman) is left seriously financially disadvantaged and with children to care for. In the case of cohabiting, unmarried, couples the disadvantage can be compounded by the lack of legal claims that reflect equality between the partners. An unmarried individual has no claim against a former cohabitant for financial assistance and property will revert to a father at the end of a child's education."

- Excerpt from Elizabeth's Politics Home article with Sir Vince Cable

The breakdown of her relationship was a bitter blow for Elizabeth after coming through a traumatic period of her life. She and her young family had moved house to help care for her father, who had lung cancer.

"While I was living there my cervical cancer was detected," says Elizabeth. "It was absolutely horrendous. My sister gave up work and moved in, and my mother had to look after my children when she had just lost her husband. I didn't know my partner had been having an affair for three years, and during my illness."

Elizabeth and her ex-partner used to run a childcare business.

"The business grew very big, very quickly into a multi-million-pound (on paper) company, but it ended in the recession," she says. "My partner resigned as a director days before it collapsed. It was horrific.

"When we moved to London I thought it was a new start for us. We moved into the houseboat and in the September I found out about the affair. It was the worst time of my life – worse than finding out I had cancer. It's had an awful impact on me and a professional has suggested I could be suffering with PTSD. I have terrible flashbacks of what my eldest son went through."

Working to stay afloat

Moses currently works part-time for Marks and Spencer, and lives with his sister, who helps him with the children.

He tried working full-time, but it became too stressful trying to balance that with bringing up his children.

"In the morning I get up with my kids, take them to breakfast club and go to work," says Moses. "The children get to spend time at school, and in the evenings I collect them from my sister, having cooked their dinner, helped them with their homework, and put them to bed. And then it is finally my relaxation time. Weekends family often help with my children. I have to be very organised.

"Financially, I'm juggling a lot of things and I'm not where I should be. I've not been able to take the children on holiday for three years.

"Childcare is a big problem for parents juggling. It's not affordable. People can't afford a nanny to cover the hours when nurseries aren't open. What you have to pay for childcare is more than you can get from benefits, so there's a gap."

Moses has an idea for a pay-as-you-go, 24-hour childcare centre, catering for parents who work shifts during the week and at weekends, particularly night-shift workers in health care, retail, manufacturing and cleaning jobs. Services – which Moses hopes would be subsidised by local councils or government – could include homework supervision, social activities, meals and overnight accommodation.

"Many people where I live work quite destabilising hours – they need time for their family and social life as well as work," he explains. "Why not utilise those different hours? If the parents are working a night shift, they can drop their children in, the children can stay overnight, they're looked after, fed, can do their homework, and you can change and have a shower there."

Until recently, Elizabeth was working as a support teacher in a local school, but she is now looking for another role that matches her qualifications and experience.

"The boys come first," she says. "I'm not able to put money aside because I have used all of my money on bringing them up by myself, and my partner has been mean with child support money. He paid child maintenance initially, albeit the bare minimum, but his contribution wasn't even enough to cover our utility bills, which suddenly became my responsibility.

"Thankfully my second son, who has severe dyslexia and ADHD, got funding for his place at a specialist school and is now in his foundation year at university. I still need to pay for his accommodation, so I do Air B&B and take in a lodger. I manage from month to month – the lodger helps a lot."

Hope on the horizon?

Despite his current situation, Moses is optimistic about the future, and is working on several different projects and ideas.

"Nothing's going to stop me," he says. "I'm not ashamed of my life. If I can use it to help other people I'm more than happy. We need to help each other. People fall through the cracks for different reasons and you have no idea of their backgrounds.

"Everyone's situation as a single parent has a different genesis. Relationships break down all the time. People need to be given realistic opportunities. I've been out of the country for a long time so I find it hard to open doors. I have got all these ideas but I need to get in front of people."

Moses is channelling his creativity into developing his ideas and projects, alongside working, parenting and volunteering as a governor at his sons' school.

"I'm writing a book about my experiences of being a single parent and an African middle-aged man in the UK," he says. "Another idea I'm working on is a TV pilot on how fatherhood has changed in the world over the last 50 years."

He adds: "I've started a new campaign called Greater Brits. It's around tribe and pride. I felt Britain had lost its way – Brits were not feeling good about themselves. We're one Britain but many Brits. It celebrates unity, diversity and inclusion. It's a multicultural society. Let's start rebuilding trust and greatness based on inclusiveness."

Elizabeth now has a supportive partner, and her youngest son is enjoying university.

"I would like to see my sons settled and happy," says Elizabeth. "My biggest wish is to see my second son graduate. I'm so proud to say that our eldest graduated last summer."

"I would love a house of my own. That's the only black cloud over me now."

In the future, she would like to spend more time on campaigning to change the law for cohabitees, and to help other mothers in her situation.

"I would hate for other mothers to have to endure what we've been through over the years," she says. "It's made our life difficult and there's no protection in this country at all."

20 Jan 2020

Number of people in poverty in working families hits record high

About 14m struggling to make ends meet.

By Phillip Inman

The proportion of people living in poverty who are in a working family has hit a record high, according to a report that shows rising levels of employment have failed to translate into higher living standards.

The Joseph Rowntree Foundation said that while paid employment reduces the risk of poverty, about 56% of people living in poverty in 2018 were in a household where at least one person had a job, compared with 39% 20 years ago.

Seven in 10 children in poverty are now in a working family, the charity's annual UK poverty report found.

Single-parent families have been the worst affected by the trend of wages falling behind living costs, it added. Working single parents accounted for three in 10 households in poverty in 2018, compared with two in 10 in 2011.

The JRF's executive director, Claire Ainsley, said the charity's latest barometer of poverty in the UK revealed the scale of the task facing Boris Johnson's administration if it is to "level up" incomes across the UK by narrowing the gap between the wealthiest cities and poorer regions.

"The new government has a historic opportunity as we enter the 2020s," she said. "Past successes in recent decades show that it is possible for the UK to loosen the grip of poverty among those most at risk, but this progress has begun to unravel, and it will take sustained effort across the country and throughout the governments of the UK to unlock poverty."

Amid concerns that the poorest receive worse healthcare and have the most insecure jobs, Ainsley said it was an indictment of recent government policy that the number of people in poverty across the whole workforce jumped from 9.9% in 1998 to 12.7% in 2018.

Labour accused the government of allowing too many people to remain trapped in lowpaid insecure work and "all too often the social security system fails to give people the support they need".

Frances O'Grady, the general secretary of the TUC, said: "The government must crack down on business models based on poverty pay and insecure jobs. Zero-hour contracts should be banned and the minimum wage must go up to at least £10 an hour right away."

More than half of people in poverty now live in a working family

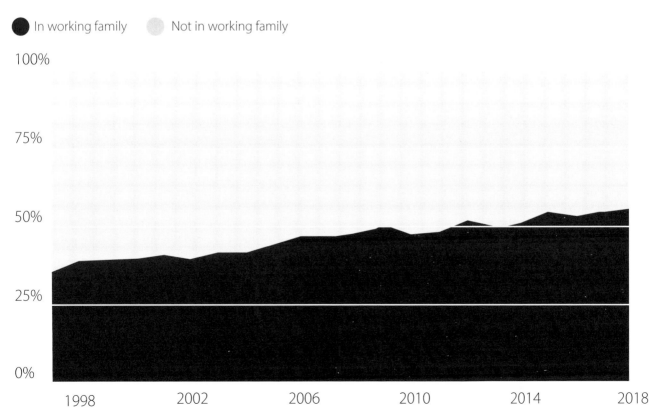

● In working family   ● Not in working family

Source: Joseph Rowntree Foundation. Financial years ending in year shown

30% of single-parent families are living in poverty

● Single with children   ● Couple with children   ● Single no children   ● Couple no children

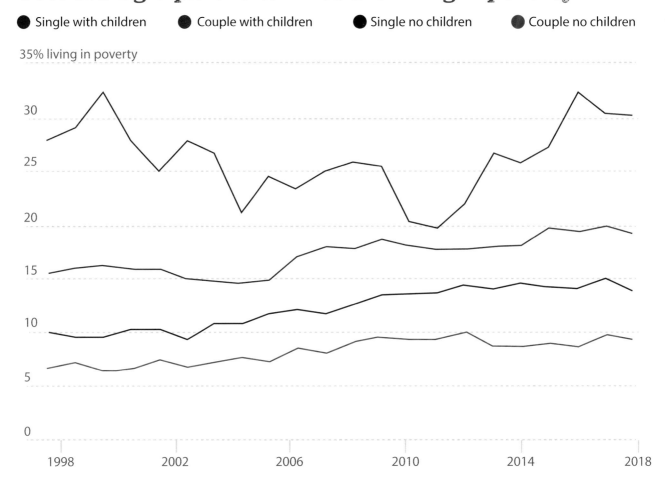

Source: Joseph Rowntree Foundation. Finanacial years ending in year shown.

Approximately 14 million people are in poverty in the UK – more than one in five of the population, including 4 million children and 2 million pensioners, up by 400,000 and 300,000 respectively over the past five years.

A family is classified as being in poverty if it has an income of less than 60% of the median income for their family type, after housing costs. A family's income includes earnings from employment, self-employment, state benefits and inheritances.

The report said people were more likely to be in poverty if they lived in certain parts of the UK, in a family where there is a disabled person or a carer, if they work in the hospitality or retail sector, or if they live in rented housing.

The worst-hit regions were London, the north of England, the Midlands and Wales, while the lowest poverty rates were found in the south of England, Scotland and Northern Ireland, the JRF said.

The charity was especially concerned about the rise in young people living with their parents, who in a previous era would have started to buy a house and start a family of their own, which it named "concealed households".

Twenty years ago, 20% (2.4 million) of 20 to 34-year-olds lived with a parent or guardian. That proportion rose to 30% in 2018, affecting 3.9 million people, the JRF found.

The report describes in-work poverty as a "critical issue for our economy" and calls for action to reduce job insecurity, lower housing costs and increase earnings for low-paid workers.

The JRF said the introduction of universal credit, which rolls six benefits into one, did not help many low-income families because it required upfront payments for childcare before households were able to access state support.

A Department for Work and Pensions spokesman said: "Tackling poverty will always be a priority for this government. We know that getting into work is the best route out of poverty – and there are more people in work than ever before. Wages are outstripping inflation and absolute poverty is lower than in 2010.

"We know that some need more help, which is why we spend over £95bn a year on working-age benefits. Millions will see their benefit payments rise further from April and we're also boosting the incomes of pensioners each year through the triple lock."

7 February 2020

Marcus Rashford highlights staggering child poverty in Bolton to win government u-turn on free meals

More than one in three children are living in poverty in the borough according to figures from the Child Poverty Action Group.

By Thomas Molloy

Manchester United and England striker Marcus Rashford referenced the levels of child poverty in some parts of Bolton as he won a stunning victory to persuade the government to provide free school meals over summer.

In an open letter, the 22-year-old asked MPs to reconsider plans to not extend the current food voucher scheme and spoke about his own experiences of receiving free school meals.

Rashford, who has raised £20m to boost food distribution with the charity FareShare, tweeted last night: "There are 2 postcodes in the Bolton South East contingency that have the level of child poverty at over 50% according to Child Poverty Action Group. 50% !! #maketheuturn."

And after the Prime Minister and Department for Education said the scheme will not be extended into the summer, the government performed a dramatic u-turn this afternoon.

A Department for Education spokesman had said: "Free schools meals are ordinarily term time only, and the national voucher scheme will not run during the summer holidays."

But at 1pm today it emerged that the government would change its mind as support grew for the campaign.

Bolton South East MP Yasmin Qureshi described Rashford's charity work with FareShare as an "incredible achievement" but said that it should "not be necessary".

She wrote: "It is a scandal in one of the richest countries in the world and I am delighted that you have stepped up your campaign to highlight this. It should not rely on the goodwill of others like you to fix this problem, but it is up to us as politicians to step up and use our power to provide long term sustainable support.

"I represent a proudly diverse community of working class people from all backgrounds.

"Bolton has high levels of child poverty with the overall rate of child poverty as of 2019 at 36.8pc after housing costs, which is 27,291 children living in poverty. The situation is worse in some areas - two postcodes in my constituency have the level of child poverty at over 50pc.

"Since the outbreak of the coronavirus, I have been contacted by countless struggling families and I have seen the same gaps in the safety net that you have highlighted in your letter.

"Many local volunteers from churches, mosques, community groups and charities have, like you, stepped up to fill the gap but they can only do so much. Community spirit is vitally important but it needs to be supported by the Government."

Mrs Qureshi added that she has written to Education Secretary Gavin Williamson to ask him to 'reconsider' and confirmed that she will continue to campaign for more support in the community to help vulnerable people.

16 June 2020

UK's austerity policy 'has driven people into poverty'

An "ideological" pursuit of austerity has replaced Britain's social safety net with a "harsh and uncaring ethos", according to the UN's special rapporteur on extreme poverty Philip Alston.

By Dominic Brady

The government has "remained determinedly in a state of denial" about the scale of poverty in the UK, Alston's scathing report for the UN, released today, has said.

"The results of the austerity experiment are crystal clear," the special rapporteur wrote in his analysis, following an official visit to the country in November 2018.

"There are 14 million people living in poverty, record levels of hunger and homelessness, falling life expectancy for some groups, ever fewer community services, and greatly reduced policing, while access to the courts for lower-income groups has been dramatically rolled back by cuts to legal aid."

He claimed local authorities throughout the country have been "abandoning" services but despite some "reluctant policy tweaks" the government has a "deeply ingrained resistance to change".

The report made a raft of recommendations including restoring local government funding to "provide critical social protection and tackle poverty at the community level", scrapping the benefits freeze and eliminating the five-week delay in receiving initial universal credit payments.

"The bottom line is that much of the glue that has held British society together since the Second World War has been deliberately removed and replaced with a harsh and uncaring ethos," Alston's report said.

Alston was particularly critical of the transformation of the benefits system under universal credit, which he said may lead to digital exclusion.

"Benefit claims are made online and the claimant interacts with authorities primarily through an online portal. The British welfare state is gradually disappearing behind a webpage and an algorithm, with significant implications for those living in poverty."

The rapporteur's findings come after a two-week mission in which he visited different regions in Great Britain and Northern Ireland. He published interim findings in November 2018 claiming that local government had been "gutted" by government policies.

He noted that close to 40% of children are predicted to be living in poverty by 2021 despite living in the fifth largest economy in the world.

"Food banks have proliferated; homelessness and rough sleeping have increased greatly; tens of thousands of poor families must live in accommodation far from their school, jobs and community networks; life expectancy is failing for certain groups; and the legal aid system has been

decimated," he added.

The Department for Work and Pensions said: "The UN's own data shows the UK is one of the happiest places in the world to live, and other countries have come here to find out more about how we support people to improve their lives.

"Therefore this is a barely believable documentation of Britain, based on a tiny period of time spent here. It paints a completely inaccurate picture of our approach to tackling poverty."

Work and pensions secretary Amber Rudd is reported to be lodging a complaint against the report. PF is awaiting confirmation on this from the Work and Pensions department.

Campbell Robb, chief executive of the poverty charity Joseph Rowntree Foundation, said: "There can be no moral justification for failing to act on this report. The picture painted by the rapporteur builds on our evidence of the 14 million people locked in poverty in the UK.

"We all want to live in a country where everyone is free to build a decent life. For too many people in the UK that is a distant dream."

Boris Johnson made inaccurate statements on child poverty, investigation finds.

By PRESS ASSOCIATION

The Government has been accused of being in denial about a rising level of child poverty in the UK.

It comes after the Office for Statistics Regulation (OSR) concluded Boris Johnson has made several inaccurate claims on the issue since being elected in December last year.

The OSR responded to a complaint from the End Child Poverty Coalition over three incidences when the Prime Minister made what the coalition described as 'misleading' statements.

Writing to the OSR, the coalition said Mr Johnson's claim on The Andrew Marr Show on December 1 2019 that there 'are 400,000 fewer children in poverty than there were in 2010' was incorrect.

It also said Mr Johnson's statement that 'absolutely poverty and relative poverty have both declined under this Government' and 'there are hundreds of thousands, I think 400,000, fewer families living in poverty now than there were in 2010', made at PMQs on June 17, this year was also untrue.

The coalition also contended that at PMQs on June 24, Mr Johnson incorrectly said 'there are 100,000 fewer children in absolute poverty and 500,000 children falling below thresholds of low income and material deprivation'.

In the letter, Anna Feuchtwang, chairwoman of the coalition, said it cannot be right that such figures are used 'selectively'.

She wrote: 'While it is expected – and right – that child poverty should be the subject of robust political debate, it cannot be right that official figures on something as fundamental as how many children are in poverty continue to be used selectively, inaccurately and, ultimately, misleadingly.'

Responding to the complaints set out in the letter, Ed Humpherson, director-general for regulation at the authority, said: 'Our team has investigated the statements which you highlight (and has reached the same conclusion that these statements are incorrect).'

Ms Feuchtwang said she welcomed the conclusion from the OSR that the Prime Minister had used child poverty statistics incorrectly.

'It is deeply insulting to the children and families swept into poverty when data about them is used selectively and misleadingly at the whim of politicians,' she said.

'The simple fact is that by any measures child poverty is rising but instead of tackling the problem the Government risks obscuring the issue and misinforming the public.

'The lives of real people are at stake and we need consistent use of information and urgent action.'

Child Poverty Action Group chief executive Alison Garnham said: 'The hard truth is that child poverty is growing in the UK but the Government is in denial on this – that has to shift.

'If we are to make progress, the problem must be confronted not circumvented.

'If the will and the focus are there, a strategy can be agreed and action taken to prevent more children from being damaged by poverty.'

She added: 'It's our moral responsibility to safeguard children from poverty and to invest in them.

'It's also the most significant investment we as a nation can make for our future.'

Imran Hussain, director of policy and campaigns at Action for Children, said that the longer the UK is in denial of the scale of child poverty, the harder it will be to fix.

'This isn't about the Punch and Judy of PMQs,' said Mr Hussain.

'Admitting that rising numbers of ordinary families are struggling to keep their children clothed and well fed matters to good policy making.

'You can't "level up" the country if you're sweeping under the carpet the big rises in child poverty clearly shown by the official figures.

'The longer we're in denial about the scale of the problem, the harder it will be to fix it.'

Shadow education secretary Kate Green said the Prime Minister must 'come clean' and correct the record on the issue.

She said: 'It is shameful that the Prime Minister is unable to tell the truth about the hardship faced by so many families struggling to make ends meet.

'Children and families in such difficult circumstances deserve better than this shabby treatment from an out-of-touch Prime Minister who has repeatedly failed to be honest about the challenges they face.

'The Prime Minister must now correct the record, both publicly and in Parliament, and ensure that when he next raises his Government's damning record on child poverty, he comes clean about what the stats are saying.'

30 July 2020

Why food banks are a cause for national pride

The Left thinks the welfare state should 'wipe away every tear'. It won't happen — and it shouldn't.

By Robin Aitken

I n his introduction to Labour's election manifesto, Jeremy Corbyn pledged to end something he called "food bank Britain", and when I read that my immediate thought was: "I hope he never does." This is not because I take any delight in the idea that thousands of my fellow citizens regularly go to local food banks to get food to feed themselves and their families, but rather because of the deeper significance of food banks; what the fact of their existence actually tells us about this country and its people. Our network of food banks should be a cause for national pride, not shame; food bank Britain is not a symptom of decline or national hard-heartedness: it shows us as our best. Let me explain.

Ten years or so ago I got involved in setting up a food bank in Oxford. It was a bit different from most food banks because, rather than receive food donations from the public to give to families in need, it set out to be a "food recovery" operation. We asked supermarkets and wholesalers to give us their surplus fresh food (bread left over at the end of the day, wilting vegetables, that sort of thing) which we then gave to other charities operating in the city. The idea quickly took off and today the organisation is a well-established part of the city's charity landscape. My involvement taught me many lessons: about the colossal (and shameful) amount of food that is wasted daily across the country but also that voluntary action, at a local level, is a good thing in and of itself. To paraphrase Shakespeare on mercy: the quality of food banks is twice blessed. It blesseth him that gives and him that takes.

In the Book of Revelation it is promised that eventually God will "wipe away every tear" and it is a long-standing fantasy of the British Left that our welfare state should emulate this feat. But there are practical reasons why this will never happen and what's more, why it should not.

One of the surprising things I learnt from my food bank experience was the appetite there is for volunteering: it was never a problem to get volunteers to drive our vans and hump around sacks of potatoes. On the contrary we often had to put volunteers on a waiting list. It's easy to sneer at "do-gooders" (and some on the Left make a speciality of it) but the instinct that drives people to offer their labour free of charge is surely a good thing. It means that individuals make a personal investment in their local community — and these are the ties which bind. A well-stocked, well-run food bank is a sign of a healthy community.

I am pretty sure that when Mr Corbyn wrote about ending food bank Britain he was not aiming his guns at local volunteer groups; what he meant, I think, was that the benefits system should be generous enough to ensure that no one need access a food bank ever again. But there are good reasons to believe that, however munificent the social security payments were, we would never arrive at that happy destination.

However hard we try there are always going to be some people in poverty; a combination of bad luck and bad individual choices will ensure it is so. Our benefits system is designed to provide a basic standard of living but despite its good intentions there are always going to be circumstances in which people don't get what they need. It is an intractable failing of a huge bureaucratic mechanism.

Food banks are a relatively new phenomenon. They burst into the national consciousness in a major way some time in the noughties and the reason they did was largely through the efforts of a charity, The Trussell Trust, which now operates about 1,200 centres across the country.

Because the work of food banks is so practical — there is, after all, no charitable action more basic and fundamental than giving

food to the poor — their appeal was immediate; kind and well-intentioned people saw food banks as a straightforward vehicle for their generosity. New food banks sprang up everywhere and because they were newcomers to the charity scene — the Trussell Trust only got going in 1997 — they attracted a lot of media attention.

Much of that media coverage was misleading. The rise in the number of food banks was used to argue that 'food poverty' was on the rise, but that was faulty logic.

Commentators and politicians said: "Look at the facts. Last year another x hundred food banks opened round the country. That proves our point." Actually the rate at which new food banks were opening was unrelated to the underlying real rate of poverty. What the statistics demonstrated was that the food bank movement had caught the public imagination; people saw them as a way of helping others in the most practical way possible. The food banks were offering a new and useful service to people on very low incomes who flocked to them. Why wouldn't they? If you are on a very tight budget a local food bank can ease the pressure. But, inevitably, food banks got dragooned into the political debate. The food bank argument is now a permanent fixture in the Left's political rhetoric. In the run-up to the election The Independent carried a story about a Tory candidate (and now MP), Darren Henry, who at a public meeting was incautious enough to offer the opinion that people who use food banks are often those who can't

manage their budgets properly. Predictably his comments were condemned by his opponents and, as the paper said, "drew gasps from the audience".

He may well be right but he would have been better advised to keep his thoughts to himself; this is an argument the Right can never win. The Independent article, in typically tendentious fashion, observed: "The proliferation of food banks, which were rare before the 2008 financial crash, has increased hugely under the Conservative government, with many experts and campaigners blaming austerity and policies such as universal credit for driving the surge in need." This is a perfect example of how the truth gets mangled in the poverty debate.

Yes, it is true that food banks were uncommon in the early years of the new millennium; that's because the movement was only just getting going. And then came the financial crash and reporters had to find a way of illustrating their stories. What better way than to highlight the growing numbers of food banks? The coverage acted as promotional videos for the food bank movement; it touched the generous instincts of the country and lo! food banks sprang up everywhere. What gets overlooked is that, had food banks been operating 30, 40 or 50 years ago they would have been just as well patronised — but then no one had thought of them.

None of this debate should obscure a fundamental truth: it is good to feed the poor.

The Church has always seen it as one of the "corporal works of mercy", that is those actions which attend to basic human necessity. It'll be a black day when Britain fails to rise to the challenge of poverty and, despite the wonders of our welfare state, there will always be the need for that to be supplemented by the efforts of individuals.

I would go further: it is neither possible, nor desirable, that the state should displace and render unnecessary all voluntary charitable action. Across the country millions of people volunteer their time and effort to help make life a little better for others. Both sides gain from this arrangement and government is well advised to let the volunteers get on with it.

While the state should never lose sight of its obligations to the poor, food banks should make us proud, not ashamed.

January 1 2020

Why the UN is investigating poverty in the UK

By John McKenna

For the past 12 days Philip Alston, the United Nation's special rapporteur on extreme poverty and human rights, has been investigating the poverty of a nation in 2018.

But the country he is investigating isn't an emerging economy. It is the United Kingdom - the fifth largest economy on the planet.

Despite rising employment levels, economic growth and pockets of enormous wealth, a fifth of Britons remain in poverty.

According to data published earlier this year, there are now 3.1 million children with working parents living in poverty in the UK. This is an extra 1 million children in poverty since 2010, in an economy that has grown by more than $220 billion over the same period.

Alston's tour of the UK took in nine towns over the 12 days, covering everything from child poverty in Glasgow to foodbanks in Newcastle, and a debate on digital exclusion at the University of Oxford.

His visit is only the second time a Western European nation has been subjected to a UN investigation into poverty, after Ireland in 2011.

Presenting the initial results of his investigation at a press conference in London on Friday, Alston blamed cuts and reforms of state benefit payments and the closure of public facilities for the poverty of 14 million people.

His findings include:

♦ 14 million people - a fifth of the UK population - live in poverty

♦ Four million of these are more than 50% below the poverty line, and 1.5 million are destitute, unable to afford basic essentials

♦ Child poverty is predicted to rise 7% between 2015 and 2022

♦ Homelessness is up 60% since 2010

♦ A 49% real terms reduction in funding for local governments since 2010

'During my visit I have spoken with people who depend on foodbanks and charities for their next meal, who are sleeping on friends' couches because they are homeless and don't have a safe place for their children to sleep, who have sold sex for money or shelter, children who are growing up in poverty unsure of their future,' Alston said.

How do we define poverty?

Definitions of poverty are split by the UN into two broad categories: extreme poverty, which is having access to less than $1 per day; and income poverty where a family's income fails to meet a government's established threshold that differs across countries.

The UK government currently has no poverty threshold in place, which has prompted the creation of an independent Social Metrics Commission to establish a new measurement of poverty for the UK.

Alston is using the benchmark of 'relative poverty', looking at the percentage of people living with less than 55% of the median income, once costs such as childcare, housing, debt and disability have been taken into account.

Food bank Britain

There are many ways of measuring the relative wealth or poverty of a nation, but the most visible indicator of rising poverty in the UK over the past decade has been the number of foodbanks appearing in church halls and community centres across the country.

Foodbanks are charitable organizations where members of the public donate food and other essentials such as toiletries, and these donations are sorted and distributed to people in need that have been referred by officials such as doctors and social workers.

The UK's largest foodbank charity, the Trussell Trust, has met with Alston during his visit to the UK.

It says more than 1.3 million people have been referred to its foodbanks for emergency food supplies over the past year - a rise of nearly 50% in just five years.

'Every week, food banks meet people referred for emergency support who have either very little income, or none at all, so we are glad to

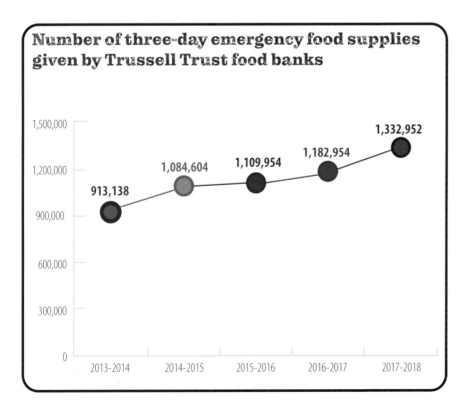

Number of three-day emergency food supplies given by Trussell Trust food banks

913,138 (2013-2014)
1,084,604 (2014-2015)
1,109,954 (2015-2016)
1,182,954 (2016-2017)
1,332,952 (2017-2018)

Primary reasons for referral to Trussell Trust food banks in 2017-2018

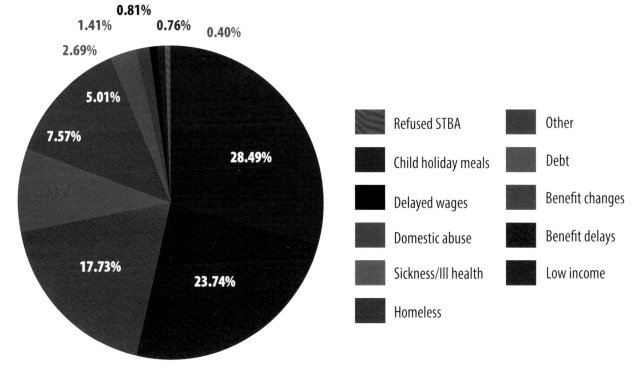

0.81%
1.41%
0.76%
0.40%
2.69%
5.01%
7.57%
28.49%
17.73%
23.74%

Legend:
- Refused STBA
- Child holiday meals
- Delayed wages
- Domestic abuse
- Sickness/Ill health
- Homeless
- Other
- Debt
- Benefit changes
- Benefit delays
- Low income

Source: The Trussell Trust

have shared the insights of our network with Philip Alston,' said Samantha Stapley, Director of Operations at the Trussell Trust.

'For too many people in the UK today, staying above water is a daily struggle. It's completely unacceptable that anyone is forced to turn to a foodbank as a result.'

Taking credit

One of the main topics of the trust's conversations with Alston was the effect of the UK government's cuts to both in-work and unemployment benefit payments.

Data from the trust shows that nearly three-quarters of referrals to their foodbanks came as the result of reductions or delays to benefit payments.

A Trussell Trust spokesman said that the particularly damaging effect of the UK government's new benefits system, called Universal Credit, was highlighted to Alston during his visit.

The charity's foodbanks in full Universal Credit rollout areas had an average increase in demand of 52% in the 12 months after the full rollout date in their area.

Comparative analysis of random samples of foodbanks taken from 247 projects either not in full Universal Credit areas, or only in full rollout areas for up to three months, showed an average increase of 13%.

Many recipients of Universal Credit, which replaces six benefits with one single monthly payment, have faced problems including underpayments and delays in payments of up to six weeks. These issues have been acknowledged by the UK government, which in its budget last month included a raft of measures to ease the transition.

Alston said the benefit reforms had a 'remarkable gender dimension' to them.

'I think if you had got a bunch of misogynists in a room and said, "Guys how can we make this system work for men, and not for women," they wouldn't have come up with too many other ideas than what's already in place,' he said.

'Ninety percent of lone parents are women, and which group do you think does absolutely the worst in the whole benefits system? Lone parents.'

Inclusive growth

Alston's visit has highlighted not only the poverty in the UK, but the growing divide in the way wealth from economic growth is distributed.

The UK's poor performance on inclusive growth was highlighted in the World Economic Forum's Inclusive Development Index 2018, where the UK ranked 21st overall.

In eight out of the 12 indicators that contribute to the index, including GDP per capita, healthy life expectancy, and wealth inequality, the UK scores in the bottom half of the rankings.

'The numbers suggest that the country is lagging behind its peers on many dimensions of inclusive growth,' says the index report.

'In particular, wealth inequality has been increasing over the past five years.'

Alston said this growing divide risked alienating large swathes of British society.

16 November 2018

The poorest countries in the world

GDP per capita is often considered an indicator of the standard of living of a given country, as it reflects the average wealth of each person residing in a country. It is therefore the standard method used to compare how poor or wealthy countries are in relation to each other. With 2018 coming to a close, we decided to take a look at our forecasts for GDP per capita from 2019 to 2023 for the 127 countries we cover to get an idea of what countries are the poorest currently and which will be making a leap toward becoming wealthier in the coming years. The projections used in this study are Consensus Forecasts based on the individual forecasts of over 1000 world renowned investment banks, economic think tanks and professional economic forecasting firms.

As one might imagine those closest to the top of the list are mostly emerging markets and least developed countries of which the majority are from Sub-Saharan Africa. Similar to our ranking for the most miserable economies, this is one of those lists where the "winners" aren't really winners; being as far from the top of the list as possible is a good thing.

Many of the poorest nations in the world are places where issues such as authoritarian regimes, political turmoil, weak financial institutions, inadequate infrastructure and corruption deter foreign investment despite the fact that many of them are immensely rich in natural resources and have a young, growing population. In our list of the top 10, five are landlocked, which means they have no direct access to maritime trade, and another one is in the midst of a civil war, which helps to explain why some of them are currently not in the best of shape.

Despite how grim that may sound, these countries stand to benefit the most in the coming years as emerging markets will become vitally important to the global economy. Although per capita GDP will still be the highest in the developed world by 2023, the fastest growth in GDP per capita will indeed come from many of the world's poorest economies currently. According to our forecasts, the highest per capita growth from 2017–2023 will be in Mongolia with an 89% increase in that time span, followed by Myanmar, Egypt, Serbia and Bangladesh with 83%, 80%, 79%, and 67% growth in per capita GDP, respectively.

With that said, let's have a look at the poorest countries in the world according to the FocusEconomics Consensus Forecast for 2019 nominal GDP per capita.

The world's poorest countries

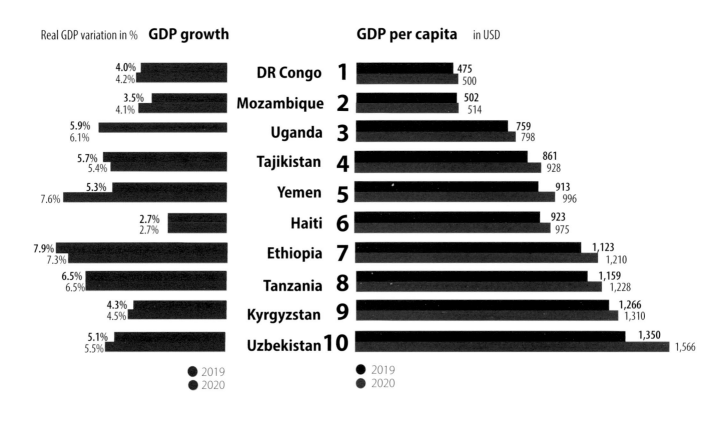

Real GDP variation in % **GDP growth**   **GDP per capita**   in USD

	GDP growth (2019 / 2020)	Rank	Country	GDP per capita (2019 / 2020)
DR Congo	4.0% / 4.2%	1		475 / 500
Mozambique	3.5% / 4.1%	2		502 / 514
Uganda	5.9% / 6.1%	3		759 / 798
Tajikistan	5.7% / 5.4%	4		861 / 928
Yemen	5.3% / 7.6%	5		913 / 996
Haiti	2.7% / 2.7%	6		923 / 975
Ethiopia	7.9% / 7.3%	7		1,123 / 1,210
Tanzania	6.5% / 6.5%	8		1,159 / 1,228
Kyrgyzstan	4.3% / 4.5%	9		1,266 / 1,310
Uzbekistan	5.1% / 5.5%	10		1,350 / 1,566

● 2019
● 2020

1. Democratic Republic of Congo

2017 GDP per Capita: USD 439
2019 GDP per Capita (projected): USD 475
2023 GDP per Capita (projected): USD 551

Although the DRC has abundant natural resources, unfortunately with a projected 2019 GDP per capita of USD 475, the country is in the unenviable position of being the poorest country in the world. There has been severe political unrest in recent years, as calls for President Joseph Kabila, who took power after the assassination of his father in 2001, to resign reached a fever pitch in 2018. Kabila was reelected in 2011 in a controversial election and has since postponed elections several times. Finally in August, Kabila declared that he would not seek re-election and named a successor candidate. The next presidential election has been slated for 23 December and opposition parties selected well-known businessman and veteran legislator, Martin Fayulu, as the unity candidate on 11 November following lengthy talks in Geneva. Fayulu has been one of the fiercest critics of President Joseph Kabila's tight grip on power. While strong activity in the extractive sectors has supported firm growth, the long-delayed elections have led to a tense business environment and a slowdown in overall activity. Moreover, Katanga Mining (a subsidiary of Glencore) announced a temporary halt to cobalt production at its Kamoto mine, after high levels of uranium were discovered.

Strong demand for key export commodities, including copper and cobalt, is expected to drive growth next year. Moreover, a sharp decline in inflation should buoy domestic demand. Political risks, however, darken the outlook. FocusEconomics analysts have thus far priced-in a peaceful transition of power—which would mark the first since independence in 1960—projecting growth of 3.7% in 2019 and 4.3% in 2020.

2. Mozambique

2017 GDP per Capita: USD 429
2019 GDP per Capita (projected): USD 502
2023 GDP per Capita (projected): USD 648

The second poorest country in the world is Mozambique with a forecasted GDP per capita of USD 502 for 2019. The former Portuguese colony has high hopes of transforming its economy based on prospects of abundant natural gas fields discovered in 2011. The country recently took an important step toward said transformation with the approval of a USD 20 billion Anadarko liquified natural gas plant in early 2018, which envisages exploiting the country's vast deposits of natural gas.

Economic growth is expected to accelerate this year on the back of higher prices for natural gas. FocusEconomics panelists see growth of 3.5% in 2019 and 4.1% in 2020.

3. Uganda

2017 GDP per Capita: USD 726
2019 GDP per Capita (projected): USD 759
2023 GDP per Capita (projected): USD 959

Uganda finds itself in third place on the list with a 2019 projected GDP per capita of USD 759. Although this represents a large leap from the level of the first two on the list, Uganda is a bit of a strange case. Following the 1986 armed conflict, the ruling political party National Resistance Movement (NRM), enacted a series of structural reforms and investments that led to a period of significant economic growth and poverty reduction all the way up to 2010. In the last five years or so, economic growth has slowed and consequently so has the pace of poverty reduction. There are a variety of factors that have brought on the slowdown, however, it has been attributed mostly to adverse weather, private sector credit constraints, the poor execution of public sector projects and unrest in their neighbor South Sudan, which has flooded the country with refugees fleeing the country and subdued exports. According to the World Bank, if Foreign Direct Investment accelerates, the banking system stabilizes, and budgeted, capital spending is executed without delays, the economy may start to pick up once again, helping to reduce poverty.

Luckily for Uganda, it appears the FDI is indeed improving according to the latest confirmed data, expanding by double digits in 2017, which bodes well for the economy and poverty reduction in the near future. The downside risk to the outlook is the weakness in the financial system, particularly the low level of credit in the private sector and the high cost of small loans. FocusEconomics panelists see growth of 5.9% in 2019 and 6.1% in 2020.

4. Tajikistan

2017 GDP per Capita: USD 777
2019 GDP per Capita (projected): USD 861
2023 GDP per Capita (projected): USD 1159

Tajikistan is number four on the list of poorest countries with a projected 2019 GDP per capita of USD 861. Tajikistan gained independence after the fall of the Soviet Union, however, a civil war broke out shortly after, which lasted five years until 1997. Since then, political stability and foreign aid have allowed the country's economy to grow, reducing poverty rather remarkably. According the World Bank, poverty fell from over 83% to 47% between 2000 and 2009 and fell further from 37% to 30% between 2012 and 2016. Since then, poverty reduction has regrettably stagnated, however, it is projected to fall from 30% to 25% by 2019 as growth picks up.

The economy, which is highly reliant on remittances, is expected to grow strongly again in 2019. Improving labor market dynamics, and a continued robust inflow of remittances supported by Russia's ongoing economic recovery, should buoy private consumption. Headwinds to the growth outlook include a less supportive external environment owing to tighter global financial conditions and the escalating tit-for-tat trade war. The economy is seen growing 5.7% in 2019 and 5.4% in 2020.

5. Yemen

2017 GDP per Capita: USD 762

2019 GDP per Capita (projected): USD 913

2023 GDP per Capita (projected): USD 1079

Yemen is in the midst of massive civil war that has caused a catastrophic humanitarian crisis, which goes a long way to explaining the country's place on this list of the poorest countries in the world. Yemen is forecast to have a GDP per capita of USD 913 in 2019.

Basic services across the country are on the verge of collapse, as half of the population is currently living in areas directly affected by the conflict and millions of Yemenis have been forcibly displaced.

Yemen is also facing the worst famine in a century, according to the United Nations, with 14 million people at risk of starvation. After peace talks failed to get off the ground in September, fighting only intensified. In recent weeks, the unofficial exchange rate has come under pressure despite a USD 200 million cash injection from Saudi Arabia into Yemen's Central Bank in October, while Yeminis around the country have protested for better living conditions.

Following three-and-a-half years of civil war, the economy is expected to return to growth for the first time in six years in 2019; albeit thanks in part to a miserably-low base effect. FocusEconomics expects the economy to expand 5.3% in 2019 and 7.6% in 2020.

6. Haiti

2017 GDP per Capita: USD 776

2019 GDP per Capita (projected): USD 923

2023 GDP per Capita (projected): USD 993

Haiti is number six on the list with an expected GDP per capita of USD 923. Haiti is extremely vulnerable to extreme weather and natural disasters with 90% of the country's population at risk according to the World Bank. These natural disasters batter the country in more ways than one, including the economy. The 2010 earthquake for example did damage equivalent to 32% of the country's GDP.

Although there is some positive sentiment over Haiti's political situation, as new president Jovenel Moïse took office in February of last year and the new parliament and cabinet were ratified later in the year, which should allow the country to accelerate reforms and move public programs forward to create a more sustainable development for all Haitians, the country remains the poorest in the Americas. More than 6 million out of 10.4 million Haitians live under the national poverty line of USD 2.41 per day and over 2.5 million live under the national extreme poverty line of USD 1.23 per day according to the latest household survey (ECVMAS 2012). As far as income equality goes, it is also one of the most unequal, with a Gini coefficient of 0.59 as of 2012.

While the economy started 2017 on a solid footing, economic activity has decelerated since, mostly due to the negative impact of Hurricanes Harvey and Irma. Furthermore, the U.S. administration's decision to scrap Temporary Protected Status (TPS) for Haitians as of July 2019 threatens all-

important remittance inflows, which account for around 34% of the country's GDP. As a result of this decision, around 60,000 Haitians currently living in the U.S. could be forced to return to Haiti.

Growth should accelerate in 2019, though the country's prospects remain hampered by rampant corruption and political instability. Growth is projected to come in at 2.7% in 2019 and 2.7% again in 2020.

7. Ethiopia

2017 GDP per Capita: USD 884

2019 GDP per Capita (projected): USD 1123

2023 GDP per Capita (projected): USD 1508

Back to Africa now with number seven on the list, Ethiopia is located in the Horn of Africa, which gives it a great strategic jumping off point, as it is close to the Middle East and its markets. Although it is technically landlocked, its tiny bordering neighbor, Djibouti, acts as its main port. Ethiopia has grown rapidly since the turn of the century, and is currently the fastest growing country in Africa, although extremely poor as evidenced by its projected 2019 GDP per capita of just USD 1123.

Along with Ethiopia's rapid economic growth came significant reductions in poverty with over 55% of Ethiopians living in extreme poverty in 2000 dropping to 33.5% in 2011, according to the World Bank. To sustain its economic growth and poverty reduction, good governance is needed, however, significant public unrest has taken hold in Ethiopia of late over the country's authoritarian regime.

In a bid to cool mass unrest and open the way for economic reforms, Prime Minister Hailemariam Desalegn submitted his resignation on 15 February. In October, parliament approved Sahle-Work Zewde to become the country's first female president —a sign of political openness from Prime Minister Abiy Ahmed. Growth should remain robust in FY 2018, although is likely to slow somewhat as the government restrains public investment growth to limit imports. That said, an improving business environment following market-friendly economic reforms could propel stronger activity in the private sector. FocusEconomics sees the economy growing 7.9% in FY 2019 and 7.3% in FY 2020.

8. Tanzania

2017 GDP per Capita: USD 1037

2019 GDP per Capita (projected): USD 1159

2023 GDP per Capita (projected): USD 1502

Number eight on the list of poorest economies is Tanzania with an expected USD 1159 GDP per capita for 2019. Tanzania's economy has been very consistent over the last decade averaging between 6 and 7% growth every year. According to the World Bank, the poverty rate has also steadily declined, however, the absolute number of people living in poverty has not due to the high growth rate of its population over that time.

Economic prospects for Tanzania depend on infrastructure investment, improving the business environment, increasing agricultural productivity, amongst others, and growth prospects for next year remain strong. The economy should continue to expand solidly, supported by sustained infrastructure spending and growth within the services sector on the back of growing tourist inflows. FocusEconomics expects GDP to expand 6.5% in 2019, which is unchanged from last month's forecast, and 6.5% in 2020.

9. Kyrgyzstan

2017 GDP per Capita: USD 1203

2019 GDP per Capita (projected): USD 1266

2023 GDP per Capita (projected): USD 1488

Kyrgyzstan is ninth on the list with an expected 2019 GDP per capita of USD 1266. A landlocked, largely mountainous country with just over 6 million inhabitants, the Kyrgyz Republic recently adopted a parliamentary system in 2011. Having experienced considerable political and social instability with weak governance and high corruption since gaining independence in 1991, the country's current democracy is a far cry from those days. Nonetheless corruption is still pervasive in the public sector, which constrain the country's economic growth potential.

The Kyrgyz economy is also vulnerable to external shocks due to its overreliance on its massive gold mine, Kumtor, which accounts for about 10% of GDP, as well as remittances, which amount to about 30% of GDP.

Growing gold production in September at the all-important Kumtor mine powered the rebound in economic activity recorded in the January–September period, when GDP increased slightly in annual terms, from the small contraction recorded in January–August. That said, cumulative mining output in January–September was still much lower than in the same period last year, which translated into falling exports. On the other hand, during the same time span, sustained wage increases and rising remittances led to a solid expansion in retail sales while both capital investment and construction increased strongly.

GDP growth is set to accelerate next year, as production at the Kumtor gold mine increases, driving output growth in the industrial sector. Solid consumer spending, fueled by healthy wage growth and higher remittances from Russia, will also underpin the expansion. A possible cooling in economic activity in Russia due to U.S. sanctions, however, cloud the outlook. FocusEconomics projects GDP growth of 4.3% in 2019 and 4.5% in 2020.

10. Uzbekistan

2017 GDP per Capita: USD 1514

2019 GDP per Capita (projected): USD 1350

2023 GDP per Capita (projected): USD 2351

Uzbekistan is last on the list of poorest countries according to 2019 GDP per capita, which is forecast to come in at USD 1350. The country's economic growth was fast between 2004 and 2016, lifting significant portions of the country out of poverty. A country rich in commodities, Uzbekistan was aided by high commodities prices and increased exports of gas, gold and copper, which generated state revenues that financed large increases in investment and wages that bolstered private consumption.

Unfortunately, in the period between 2013 and 2016, commodities prices came crashing down along with the weak performance of Russia and China, key trade partners, adversely affected the economy. Despite the external environment weakening, the government's countercyclical fiscal and monetary policies allowed growth to slow only slightly, however, poverty reduction has largely stagnated.

In February of 2017, the government began implementing its Strategy of Actions for the Development of Uzbekistan for 2017-2021, which among other things included measures to liberalize its economy. One measure was implemented in September of 2017, which linked the official exchange rate with the curb market rate and established a framework to allow it to flow.

The economy moderated sharply in 2017 to 5.3% from 2016's 7.8%, the slowest point since 2003. The moderation partly reflected the impact of the currency devaluation, which had caused inflation to spike and real disposable income to drop. It also underscored the short-lived impact that many market-friendly reforms pushed ahead by the government to attract foreign investment are having on the economy.

The economy grew 5.2% annually in the January–September 2018 period, driven by a strong services sector and solid industrial output. Industrial activity was propped up by soaring mining and quarrying production, largely thanks to a booming natural gas sector. In addition, construction activity expanded robustly in the same period, supported by buoyant demand for real estate amid easing inflationary pressures. On 19 October, authorities began preparatory work on the country's first nuclear plant, estimated to cost USD 11 billion and largely financed by Russia, in a bid to further strengthen Uzbekistan's energy sector. The government has also signed multibilliondollar economic and investment deals with Russia and the U.S. as the country continues its pro-liberal economic policy push.

In 2019, growth should remain solid on the back of sustained government spending, healthy capital investment and a growing inflow of remittances from Russia. FocusEconomics expects the economy to expand 5.1% in 2019, down 0.4 percentage points from last month's forecast, and 5.5% in 2020.

19 November 2018

The poorest 20% of Americans are richer on average than most European nations

The privilege of living in the US affords poor people more material resources than the averages for most of the world's richest nations.

By James D.Agresti

A ground-breaking study by Just Facts has discovered that after accounting for all income, charity, and non-cash welfare benefits like subsidized housing and food stamps, the poorest 20 percent of Americans consume more goods and services than the national averages for all people in most affluent countries. This includes the majority of countries in the prestigious Organization for Economic Cooperation and Development (OECD), including its European members. In other words, if the US 'poor' were a nation, it would be one of the world's richest.

Notably, this study was reviewed by Dr. Henrique Schneider, professor of economics at Nordakademie University in Germany and the chief economist of the Swiss Federation of Small and Medium-Sized Enterprises. After examining the source data and Just Facts' methodology, he concluded: 'This study is sound and conforms with academic standards. I personally think it provides valuable insight into poverty measures and adds considerably to this field of research.'

The 'poorest' rich nation?

In a July 1 New York Times video op-ed that decries 'fake news' and calls for 'a more truthful approach' to 'the myth of America as the greatest nation on earth,' Times producers Taige Jensen and Nayeema Raza claim the US has 'fallen well behind Europe' in many respects and has 'more in common with "developing countries" than we'd like to admit.'

'One good test' of this, they say, is how the US ranks in the OECD, a group of '36 countries, predominantly wealthy, Western, and Democratic.' While examining these rankings, they corrupt the truth in ways that violate the Times' op-ed standards, which declare that 'you can have any opinion you would like,' but 'the facts in a piece must be supported and validated,' and 'you can't say that a certain battle began on a certain day if it did not.'

The Times is not merely wrong about this issue but is also reporting the polar opposite of reality.

A prime example is their claim that 'America is the richest country' in the OECD, 'but we're also the poorest, with a whopping 18% poverty rate – closer to Mexico than Western Europe.' That assertion prompted Just Facts to conduct a rigorous, original study of this issue with data from the OECD, the World Bank, and the US government's Bureau of Economic Analysis. It found that the Times is not merely wrong about this issue but is also reporting the polar opposite of reality.

Poor compared to whom?

The most glaring evidence against the Times' rhetoric is a note located just above the OECD's data for poverty rates. It explains that these rates measure relative poverty within nations, not between nations. As the note states, the figures represent portions of people with less than 'half the median household income' in their own nations and thus 'two countries with the same poverty rates may differ in terms of the relative income-level of the poor.'

The OECD's poverty rates say nothing about which nation is 'the poorest.' Nonetheless, this is exactly how the Times misrepresented them.

The upshot is laid bare by the fact that this OECD measure assigns a higher poverty rate to the US (17.8 percent) than to Mexico (16.6 percent). Yet World Bank data show that 35 percent of Mexico's population lives on less than $5.50 per day, compared to only 2 percent of people in the United States.

Hence, the OECD's poverty rates say nothing about which nation is 'the poorest.' Nonetheless, this is exactly how the Times misrepresented them.

The same point applies to broader discussions about poverty, which can be measured in two very different ways: (1) relative poverty or (2) absolute poverty. Relative measures of poverty, like the one cited by the Times, can be misleading if the presenter does not answer the question: Poor compared to who? Absolute measures, like the number of people with income below a certain level, are more straightforward and enlightening.

Unmeasured income and benefits

To accurately compare living standards across or within nations, it is necessary to account for all major aspects of material welfare. None of the data above does this.

The OECD data is particularly flawed because it is based on 'income,' which excludes a host of non-cash government benefits and private charity that are abundant in the United States. Examples include but are not limited to:

◆ Health care provided by Medicaid, free clinics, and the Children's Health Insurance Program.

◆ Nourishment provided by food stamps, school lunches, school breakfasts, soup kitchens, food pantries, and the Women's, Infants' & Children's program.

- Housing and amenities provided through rent subsidies, utility assistance, and homeless shelters.

The World Bank data includes those items but is still incomplete because it is based on government 'household surveys,' and US low-income households greatly underreport both their income and non-cash benefits in such surveys. As documented in a 2015 paper in the Journal of Economic Perspectives entitled 'Household Surveys in Crisis':

- In recent years, more than half of welfare dollars and nearly half of food stamp dollars have been missed in several major government surveys.

- There has been 'a sharp rise' in the underreporting of government benefits received by low-income households in the United States.

- This 'understatement of incomes' masks 'the poverty-reducing effects of government programs' and leads to 'an overstatement of poverty and inequality.'

Likewise, the US Bureau of Economic Analysis explains that such surveys 'have issues with recalling income and expenditures and are subject to deliberate underreporting of certain items.' The US Census Bureau says much the same, writing that 'for many different reasons there is a tendency in household surveys for respondents to underreport their income.'

There is also a wider lesson here. When politicians and the media talk about income inequality, they often use statistics that fail to account for large amounts of income and benefits received by low- and middle-income households. This greatly overstates inequality and feeds deceptive narratives.

Relevant, reliable data

The World Bank's 'preferred' indicator of material well-being is 'consumption' of goods and services. This is due to 'practical reasons of reliability and because consumption is thought to better capture long-run welfare levels than current income.' Likewise, as a 2003 paper in the Journal of Human Resources explains:

- 'Research on poor households in the U.S. suggests that consumption is better reported than income' and is 'a more direct measure of material well-being.'

- 'Consumption standards were behind the original setting of the poverty line,' but governments now use income because of its 'ease of reporting.'

The World Bank publishes a comprehensive dataset on consumption that isn't dependent on the accuracy of household surveys and includes all goods and services, but it only provides the average consumption per person in each nation—not the poorest people in each nation.

However, the US Bureau of Economic Analysis published a study that provides exactly that for 2010. Combined with World Bank data for the same year, these datasets show that the poorest 20 percent of US households have higher average consumption per person than the averages for all people in most nations of the OECD and Europe:

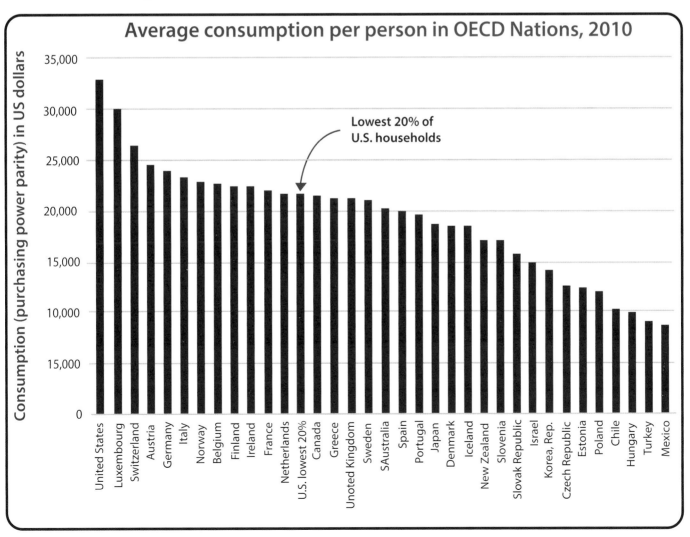

Average consumption per person in OECD Nations, 2010

The high consumption of America's 'poor' doesn't mean they live better than average people in the nations they outpace, like Spain, Denmark, Japan, Greece, and New Zealand. This is because people's quality of life also depends on their communities and personal choices, like the local politicians they elect, the violent crimes they commit, and the spending decisions they make.

For instance, a Department of Agriculture study found that US households receiving food stamps spend about 50 percent more on sweetened drinks, desserts, and candy than on fruits and vegetables. In comparison, households not receiving food stamps spend slightly more on fruits & vegetables than on sweets.

> ## The fact remains that the privilege of living in the US affords poor people more material resources than the averages for most of the world's richest nations.

Nonetheless, the fact remains that the privilege of living in the US affords poor people more material resources than the averages for most of the world's richest nations.

Another important strength of this data is that it is adjusted for purchasing power to measure tangible realities like square feet of living area, foods, smartphones, etc. This removes the confounding effects of factors like inflation and exchange rates. Thus, an apple in one nation is counted the same as an apple in another.

To spot-check the results for accuracy, Just Facts compared the World Bank consumption figure for the entire US with the one from the Bureau of Economic Analysis. They were within 2 percent of each other.

In light of these facts, the Times' claim that the US has 'more in common with developing countries than we'd like to admit' is especially far-fetched. In 2010, even the poorest 20 percent of Americans consumed three to 30 times more goods and services than the averages for all people in a wide array of developing nations around the world.

These immense gaps in standards of living are a major reason why people from developing nations immigrate to the US instead of vice versa.

Why is the US so much richer?

Instead of maligning the United States, the Times could have covered this issue in a way that would help people around the world improve their material well-being by

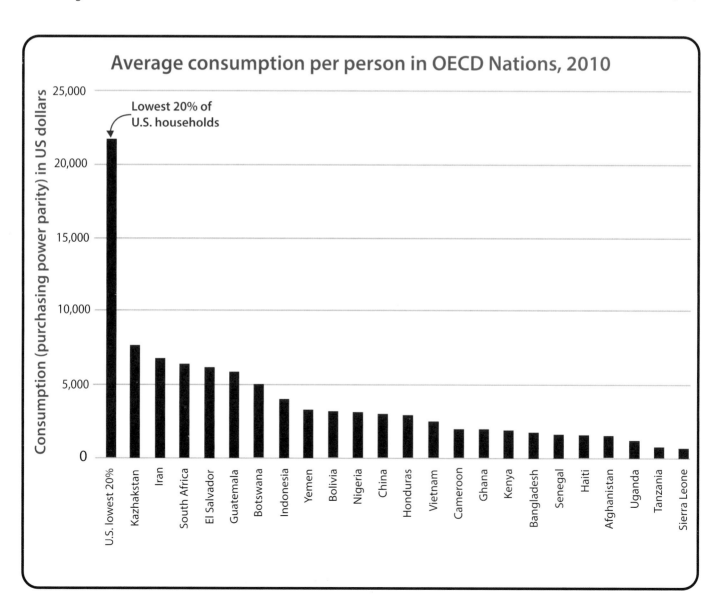

Average consumption per person in OECD Nations, 2010

replicating what makes the US so successful. However, that would require conveying the following facts, many of which the Times has previously misreported:

♦ High energy prices, like those caused by ambitious 'green energy' programs in Europe, depress living standards, especially for the poor.

♦ High tax rates reduce incentives to work, save, and invest, and these can have widespread harmful effects.

♦ Abundant social programs can reduce market income through multiple mechanisms—and as explained by President Obama's former chief economist Lawrence Summers, 'government assistance programs' provide people with 'an incentive, and the means, not to work.'

♦ The overall productivity of each nation trickles down to the poor, and this is partly why McDonald's workers in the US have more real purchasing power than in Europe and six times more than in Latin America, even though these workers perform the same jobs with the same technology.

♦ Family disintegration driven by changing attitudes toward sex, marital fidelity, and familial responsibility has strong, negative impacts on household income.

♦ In direct contradiction to the Times, a wealth of data suggests that aggressive government regulations harm economies.

Many other factors correlate with the economic conditions of nations and individuals, but the above are some key ones that give the US an advantage over many European and other OECD countries.

'The truth is worth it'

In reality, the US is so economically exceptional that the poorest 20 percent of Americans are richer than many of the world's most affluent nations.

The Times closes its video by claiming that 'America may once have been the greatest, but today America, we're just okay.' In reality, the US is so economically exceptional that the poorest 20 percent of Americans are richer than many of the world's most affluent nations.

Last year, the Times adopted a new slogan: 'The truth is worth it.' Yet, in this case, and others, it has twisted the truth in ways that can genuinely hurt people. The Times makes other spurious claims about the US in this same video, which will be deflated in future articles.

30 August 2019

Chart of the day: these countries have seen the biggest falls in extreme poverty

By Rosamond Hutt

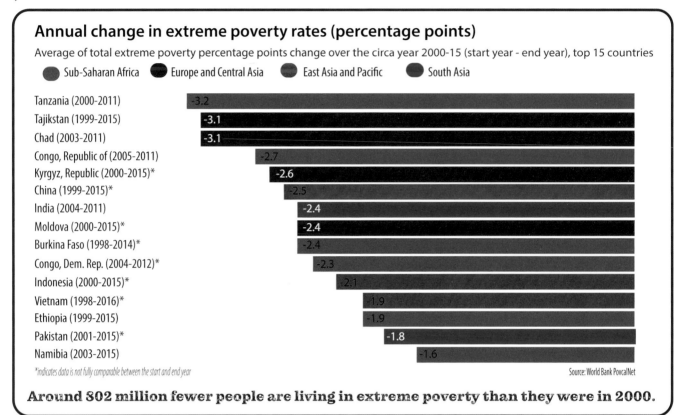

Annual change in extreme poverty rates (percentage points)

Average of total extreme poverty percentage points change over the circa year 2000-15 (start year - end year), top 15 countries

● Sub-Saharan Africa ● Europe and Central Asia ● East Asia and Pacific ● South Asia

Tanzania (2000-2011)	-3.2
Tajikstan (1999-2015)	-3.1
Chad (2003-2011)	-3.1
Congo, Republic of (2005-2011)	-2.7
Kyrgyz, Republic (2000-2015)*	-2.6
China (1999-2015)*	-2.5
India (2004-2011)	-2.4
Moldova (2000-2015)*	-2.4
Burkina Faso (1998-2014)*	-2.4
Congo, Dem. Rep. (2004-2012)*	-2.3
Indonesia (2000-2015)*	-2.1
Vietnam (1998-2016)*	-1.9
Ethiopia (1999-2015)	-1.9
Pakistan (2001-2015)*	-1.8
Namibia (2003-2015)	-1.6

indicates data is not fully comparable between the start and end year

Source: World Bank PovcalNet

Around 802 million fewer people are living in extreme poverty than they were in 2000.

♦ About 1.1 billion people have moved out of extreme poverty since 1990.

♦ 15 countries have made rapid progress in reducing extreme poverty.

♦ Tanzania almost halved its extreme poverty in just over a decade.

♦ China, Kyrgyz Republic, Moldova and Vietnam effectively ended extreme poverty by 2015.

An estimated 1.1 billion people have lifted themselves out of extreme poverty in just a few decades.

By 2015, according to the most recent data, 736 million people, or about 10% of the world's population, were living in extreme poverty, which the World Bank defines as living on the equivalent of $1.90 or less per day. That's down from 1.85 billion people in 1990.

However, some countries have experienced more success than others in reducing rates of extreme poverty – China being the most obvious example.

In the past 40 years, China has taken more than 850 million citizens out of extreme poverty.

This chart shows the remarkable progress of 15 countries on cutting extreme poverty,

Across these 15 countries, an average of 1.6% of the population moved out of extreme poverty every year between about 2000 and 2015. This equates to around 802 million fewer people living in extreme poverty during that period.

Tanzania almost halved its extreme poverty rate between 2000 and 2011. It fell by an average of 3.2 percentage points per year, and Tajikistan and Chad weren't far behind with 3.1 percentage points.

About 86% of the Tanzanian population were living in extreme poverty in 2000, down to 49.1% by 2011.

Four of the 15 countries – China, Kyrgyz Republic, Moldova, and Vietnam – managed to eradicate extreme poverty altogether.

Uneven progress

But although the world has made huge progress on extreme poverty reduction, progress hasn't been even.

The majority of the 736 million people still living on less than $1.90 a day are in sub-Saharan Africa. Even among sub-Saharan high-performers such as Tanzania, rates of extreme poverty remain above 40%.

In addition, the pace of decline in the overall extreme poverty rate has slowed since 2013, and the world isn't on track to hit the target of ending poverty by 2030.

9 March 2020

Child poverty

- 663 million children worldwide – nearly one in three – live in poverty
- 385 million children are living in extreme poverty, forced to survive on less than $1.90 a day
- Children are more than twice as likely to live poverty than adults
- Children from the poorest households die at twice the rate of their better-off peers

In recent years, the world has made remarkable strides advancing development. Yet, some 736 million people still live in extreme poverty. Children are disproportionately affected. Despite comprising one third of the global population, they represent half of those struggling to survive on less than $1.90 a day.

Children who grow up impoverished often lack the food, sanitation, shelter, health care and education they need to survive and thrive. Across the world, about one in three children – roughly 663 million – live in households that are multidimensionally poor, meaning they lack necessities as basic as nutrition or clean water.

An estimated 385 million children live in extreme poverty.

The consequences are grave. Worldwide, the poorest children are twice as likely to die in childhood than their wealthier peers. For those growing up in humanitarian crises, the risks of deprivation and exclusion surge. Even in the world's richest countries, one in seven children still live in poverty. Today, one in four children in the European Union are at risk of falling into poverty.

No matter where they are, children who grow up impoverished suffer from poor living standards, develop fewer skills for the workforce, and earn lower wages as adults.

Yet, only a limited number of Governments have set the elimination of child poverty as a national priority.

UNICEF's response

Child poverty is neither inevitable nor immune to efforts to address it. As many countries have already shown, it can be reduced and even eradicated through continued attention and action.

With the Sustainable Development Goals (SDGs), nations agreed for the first time in history to end extreme child poverty. The SDGs call for multidimensional child poverty – a measure of poverty that goes beyond income – to be halved by 2030, building a world in which all children have what they need to survive, thrive and fulfil their potential.

As part of this commitment, UNICEF mobilizes actors at the national, regional and global levels to help countries measure and address child poverty in all its dimensions. With the World Bank, we produce global statistics on extreme child poverty that help guide policymakers. We also work with Governments and partners on integrated policies and programmes, backed by the resources needed to put them into practice. Our efforts support the expansion of child-sensitive social protection programmes, including universal child benefits, which have been shown to positively impact children's health, education and nutrition.

Since 2014, UNICEF has played an instrumental role in directing global attention to child poverty. The Global Coalition to End Child Poverty, chaired by UNICEF, has become a powerful initiative for raising awareness about child poverty and accelerating global efforts to tackle it.

2020

Rwanda invests in model villages to tackle poverty

Rwanda is expanding a rural development program that is slashing poverty, but at the expense of free choice. Are the benefits worth it?

By Tara Heidger

Rwanda is tackling poverty through a controversial rural development program that the government plans to expand aggressively in coming years.

Over the last decade, more than 4,000 Rwandan families have been resettled into model villages. The villages feature three-bedroom brick homes equipped with water, solar panels and sanitation systems, along with social and economic infrastructure.

Rwanda is now expanding the model village program. The government's goal is to have 70% of the population living in an urban area or village by 2024.

Rwanda is the fifth most densely populated country in the world and the most densely populated in Africa, with 512 people per square kilometer. The hilly terrain and increasingly short supply of land make it difficult to deliver roads, sewers and electrical infrastructure to thousands of scattered farming settlements.

The government sees the movement of people into villages as a way to improve access to public infrastructure and to lift much of the rural population out of poverty.

Model villages are typically home to 200-500 people and can cover five to 10 hectares of land (one hectare is roughly the size of a 400-meter racetrack). Government ministries determine where model villages will be located, taking account of land, development, local government and infrastructure conditions.

The government already owns some of the land devoted to the model villages. In other cases, the government uses its expropriation powers to buy private property.

People are not given a choice about relocation.

This isn't always a smooth process. A 2017 Human Rights Watch report said a number of Rwandan families were forcibly removed by authorities to make way for a model village. Those who were displaced said their rights to fair compensation and public consultation were ignored.

According to Rwanda's Ministry of Finance and Economic Planning, the 2019/2020 budget has allocated US$31 million to rural development projects, up from $9 million the year before — a 244% increase in spending.

The budget outlines the Rwanda government's intention to relocate 32,000 of the 455,000 isolated rural households nationwide by 2021. The majority of funding for these projects will come from domestic revenues; international development funds would provide 16%.

Local governments determine who will live in each village. They work off a list of the districts' most vulnerable people. The vulnerability standards are set yearly and based on a process called *ubudehe*, where households are ranked by the community to determine each family's level of poverty based on assets, quality of living structure, disability, gender and the extent to which they were affected by Rwanda's genocide of 1994.

In some areas, residents vulnerable to landslides — which are commonplace in a mountainous land — get priority.

Residents are granted ownership after five years.

A district committee made up of locally-elected leaders and their staff determine individuals' eligibility. Once selected, people are not given a choice about relocation. Those who refuse to move are ostracized by the government and cut off from social support until they comply.

The biggest challenge to the model village program is addressing the cultural mindset of the rural population, said John Twahirwa of the Rwandan Housing Authority in Kigali. Moving from the country to a village is difficult, even with the lure of water and electricity and the prospect of owning a nice home.

Under Rwanda's land tenure laws, new residents are granted ownership of the land and house after five years of occupancy. A contract between the tenant and the district leadership requires that the home be occupied by the designated tenant for five years and not rented out.

Public sentiment about the mandatory moves is mixed.

In interviews with more than 15 recently resettled families, most said they were grateful to have large homes equipped with electricity and running water and access to nearby schools and clinics. One family noted their children no longer risked being burned by candlelight and were able to be more productive after sunset.

Villagization has a long history.

Others were frustrated by the distance they were now required to travel to farm their land — in some cases, further than the five kilometers recommended by the Model Village Program guidelines.

'For the first time in our lives, we have electricity, but no food,' said one elderly couple who became eligible for the program due to their poverty and genocide survivor status. They had previously lived in a rented, thatched-roof home near family and were now far from relatives and sources of support. They now rely on their new neighbors and handouts from local churches for food.

The implementation of model villages — sometimes called villagization — has a long history in sub-Saharan Africa. Human rights groups criticized similar efforts by Ethiopia and Tanzania in the 1980s that resulted in more than 12 million people being forced to move, saying violent and forced relocations resulted in significant rights abuses.

But projects in Ghana, Malawi and Uganda had more positive results, including an increase in school attendance and improved health indicators — potentially due to the projects' international implementation and oversight.

While it is too early to discern the long-term effects of Rwanda's program to alleviate poverty, the early indications are that rural poverty has eased.

A 2019 United Nations report on Rwanda's implementation of its sustainable development goals said the number of Rwandans living below the national poverty line fell from 60% to 38% between 2001 and 2017, while the country achieved all but one of the UN Millennium Development Goals.

Much of the progress has stemmed from efforts outside of the rural development sector. But ensuring homes, infrastructure and social support are available through programs such as the model village program will likely continue to have a lasting impact.

13 November 2019

THREE QUESTIONS TO CONSIDER:

♦ What is 'villagization?'

♦ Why is Rwanda's rural development program controversial?

♦ Do you think governments should disregard individuals' preferences for the sake of achieving an admirable policy goal like poverty alleviation?

Why taxing wealth more effectively can help to reduce inequality and poverty

By Oliver Pearce

Since 2014, Oxfam's Even It Up campaign has been pressing governments to tackle economic inequality because it is hindering efforts to end poverty. Recent World Bank estimates show that according to current economic growth predictions – and if present levels of inequality remain unchanged – in 2030 about 6.5% of the global population will still be living in extreme poverty. Tackling inequality to reduce each country's Gini index by 1% per year would reduce extreme poverty more than increasing its annual growth rate by one percentage point above forecasts.

Further, International Monetary Fund economists have found that inequality both hampers the power of growth to reduce poverty and diminishes the robustness of growth. Lower inequality tends to be associated with faster and more durable growth.

As noted by former World Bank chief economist Francois Bourguignon, redistribution through taxation and spending policies might achieve: 'not only greater equality but also faster growth, and for developing economies, faster poverty reduction'.

Wealth inequality is more acute than income inequality. Last year the wealth of the world's billionaires grew by $2.5bn a day – or around 12%, whilst the combined wealth of the poorest half of humanity fell by 11%. One of the reasons is that – as economists including Thomas Piketty have pointed out– returns to capital tend to outstrip the rate of economic growth, so those who have capital can become richer more quickly than those whose main income is from labour.

In addition, wealth inequality entrenches privilege at the top and limits equality of opportunity. The richest can benefit from returns on wealth such as profits on investments or property, unlike those at the bottom. The wealthiest may also be able to use their money and power to influence government policies to reflect their interests.

Wealth is often under-taxed

This trend is exacerbated by most governments' approach to taxing wealth. Globally, just four pence in every pound of tax revenue collected in 2015 came from taxes on wealth such as inheritance or property. For most forms of wealth in most countries, the rate of tax on capital gains or other forms of wealth taxes is much lower than equivalent tax rates on labour. This helps to entrench the high returns to capital, exacerbating wealth inequality. The UK is no exception, with tax rates on capital gains set at 10% (for basic rate taxpayers) or 20% (for higher rate taxpayers), significantly below the equivalent personal income tax rates of 20% or 40% (or 45%).

There is growing support for better use of wealth taxes to tackle inequality. The outgoing head of the IMF, Christine Lagarde, has proposed using wealth taxes to tackle inter-generational inequality. International economists on the right as well as the left have suggested how wealth could be taxed more effectively – with options including a land tax – in order to address acute wealth inequality and raise extra revenue for governments to invest in public services and poverty reduction without harming growth.

Another proposal from the Institute on Fiscal Studies is that governments consider taxing the returns to wealth at the same level as income from labour. Such a change would help to arrest growing wealth inequality as well as raise revenue in a fairer way.

Another option governments can consider is a net wealth tax, which could be less distortionary than other kinds of tax. Although some governments have moved away from this model, current net wealth taxes in Spain, Switzerland and Norway appear to be working well and have reasonably broad support. Whilst the design of specific taxes can be no doubt be improved, such taxes raise important revenue, help to address wealth inequality and send a signal that governments are committed to creating fairer economies.

Bill Gates and Warren Buffet have called for higher taxes on wealth, and US billionaires including George Soros, Chris Hughes (co-founder of Facebook) and heiress Abigail Disney recently urged presidential candidates to back a wealth tax on the richest Americans to create a more equal society.

Cracking down on tax avoidance

Although most wealth taxes should be progressive because the amount of tax due should be linked to the amount of wealth someone owns, very wealthy individuals may be able to avoid them by employing accountants who can advise them on how to move wealth offshore or into assets that are harder to identify. Properly structured wealth taxes could help to address this, and would have to come alongside concerted action to tackle tax dodging. Oxfam supports the idea put forward by leading economists including Nobel Prize winner Joseph Stiglitz, Thomas Piketty and Gabriel Zucman to see how a global asset registry could be implemented, which would mean tax officials can see who owns what wealth around the world. Already, improved technology and greater exchange of information between governments on tax-related data is making it harder for individuals to hide assets offshore than in recent years.

Oxfam and others have also long been calling for transparency in tax havens, including public registers of beneficial ownership, to help ensure that governments of countries rich and poor can claim the revenue they are due.

Reforming wealth taxes in the UK

In the UK our wealth taxes are relatively regressive, as the Institute for Public Policy Research has shown, mainly because Council Tax, which makes up the largest proportion, is not progressive: poorer people pay a relatively higher proportion of their incomes on Council Tax. The UK raises slightly more of its tax revenue than most other countries from wealth taxes, but as a proportion this remains low – about 4% of GDP compared to 15% from taxes on income and 11% from consumption. Recent changes such as a higher threshold for income tax and cutting capital gains and corporate tax rates have tended to make the UK's tax system overall less progressive.

There is growing support for reforming UK wealth taxes to make them fairer from across the political spectrum, with various options being proposed. For example, the IPPR Commission on Economic Justice, which includes the Archbishop of Canterbury and senior business figures, has called for 'a transformation of the tax treatment of wealth in the UK' in order to create a more equal society, including an annual property tax, a land value tax, and a lifetime donee-based gift tax.

Former Conservative minister Lord David Willets, now chair of the Resolution Foundation, says a tax on wealth is needed to tackle rising levels of inequality between young and old. The Resolution Foundation has calculated that almost £7 billion a year could be raised by "tightening up" existing wealth taxes and subsidies.

IFS Director Paul Johnson argues that the UK's current system of wealth taxes could be fairer and raise more money, for example by changing council tax so it's proportional to the current value of the property, a form of land value tax, and closing obvious loopholes in the capital gains and inheritance tax systems. Bank of England former deputy governors Rachel Lomax and Sir Charles Bean have said governments should consider taxing wealth better, and property in particular, to reduce the need for higher government borrowing.

Further ideas for consideration are aligning the rates on capital gains with income tax; and perhaps a net wealth tax. By way of illustration, Oxfam has calculated that a net wealth tax based on Spain's model could raise about £10 billion a year, and reduce the UK's Gini coefficient by around 1 per cent.

Time to tax wealth more effectively

To illustrate the magnitude of revenue that could be harnessed through a small increase in taxing wealth globally, Oxfam estimated it would only take a small increase (0.5% of the value of net wealth on the wealthiest 1% of people in each country) to raise sufficient revenue to ensure that every child goes to school and no one is bankrupted by the cost of medical treatment for their families. Thinking about wealth taxes in this way shows that small taxes on those holding significant wealth could not only help reduce inequality in itself, but also be put to powerful use to further close the rich-poor divide through funding public services.

Oxfam has developed policy recommendations on different wealth taxes that could be used to help reduce inequality and raise funds to fight poverty (for example inheritance, property, capital gains, net wealth taxes) which colleagues around the world adapt to domestic contexts. For example, colleagues in India, where the top 10% of the population own almost three quarters of all wealth, have contributed to a major tax reform process by analysing how the tax system could be more progressive and raise additional revenue to invest in much-needed social services.

Many countries are already managing to raise significant resources in a fair way by taxing wealth, so this comes down to political will. Governments can decide to use wealth taxes more effectively, at the same time raising more revenue for fighting poverty and inequality-busting public services. Rich countries can also use some of the extra revenue raised from wealth taxes to contribute to development aid for tackling climate change, and investment in vital public services which help to reduce gender and economic inequality.

22 August 2019

10 solutions to global poverty that can be implemented today

By Chylene Babb

Nearly half of the world's population lives at or below the poverty line; out of the 2.2 billion children in the world, one billion of them live in poverty. Though this issue may not be as prevalent or visible in the U.S., it is an issue that affects everyone. Small steps can be taken to better this problem, leading to possible solutions to global poverty.

1. Properly identifying issues

One of the largest issues involving poverty is the inability to properly identify contributing factors at the micro and macro level. Many organizations assume that local aid alone will better the problem, but it is only with the combined efforts of local, state and national governments that poverty will lessen.

2. Allocating proper time and resources

Preventable diseases such as pneumonia claim the lives of nearly two million children per year. Without proper planning, which includes allocating enough time, money and volunteer work, global poverty will continue to exist. Currently, the U.S. spends only about one percent of the federal budget on foreign aid. By creating detailed plans and projects aimed at helping other nations, global poverty will begin to lessen.

3. Creating organizations and communities to work locally

Enacting policy is not the only solution to global poverty, as policy often does not affect those suffering directly. As previously stated, efforts must come from both local and federal domains. Essentially, while policy is created to change legislation, local organizations enact the changes, directly helping those in need.

On top of that, working with entire communities instead of specific individuals has been proven to be more effective.

4. Creating jobs

Creating jobs in poverty-ridden communities allows individuals to pull themselves out of poverty. This solution to global poverty is arguably one of the most effective.

Federal governments can achieve this by rebuilding their infrastructures, developing renewable energy sources, renovating abandoned housing and raising the minimum wage.

5. Raising the minimum wage

By raising the minimum wage in existing jobs, companies would combat recent inflation in both developed and developing countries. This change in the states (in places

such as Seattle and Washington) has been shown to reduce poverty.

6. Providing access to healthcare

Unpaid medical bills are the leading cause of bankruptcy. Having access to free or affordable healthcare would allow families to allocate the money they would normally spend on healthcare elsewhere.

7. Empowering women

Female empowerment in developing countries often comes from organizations that work to reduce poverty by allowing them to take leadership positions and advance socially and economically.

8. Microfinancing

Microfinancing provides improvements to socioeconomic status by providing access to more, larger loans, providing better repayment rates for women, as they are less likely to default on their loans than men, and extending education programs for loan-payers' children. It can also improve health and welfare by providing access to clean water and better sanitation, create new jobs and teach developing countries to be more sustainable.

Microfinancing continues to prove that even the smallest amounts of credit can be one of the many solutions to global poverty.

9. Provide paid leave and paid sick days

Paid maternal and paternal leave allows families to save money after childbirth, as having a child is a leading cause of economic hardship. Furthermore, giving workers paid sick days allows them to properly get over their illness without worrying about missing a paycheck or receiving a paycheck with fewer funds than normal.

10. Supporting equal pay for men and women

Closing the wage gap between men and women would reduce 50 percent of poverty experienced by women and their families. This would also add money to the nation's gross domestic product.

Global poverty has proven to be an unruly, frustrating cycle, but eradicating it is within our means. These solutions to global poverty can and should be implemented to begin the end of poverty.

30 March 2018

Coronavirus is pushing people into poverty – but temporary basic income can stop this

An article from The Conversation.

By Eduardo Ortiz-Juarez

THE CONVERSATION

The rapid spread of COVID-19 across developing countries has led to a devastating loss of life and livelihoods. The pandemic is having both immediate economic effects and long-lasting consequences on development. This is because developing economies are less able to handle shocks than advanced ones.

Around 80% of workers in developing countries are engaged in tasks that are unlikely to be performed from home, meaning lockdowns are preventing them from working. And 70% of workers make a living in informal markets, with the majority not being covered by any form of social protection. COVID-19 containment measures are leaving a large number of people without any income.

Global poverty has fallen over the past three decades, but many of those lifted out of it have remained vulnerable. They sit just above the poverty line, but are ineligible for existing anti-poverty cash assistance. In a previous article, my co-authors and I argued that this could lead to an increase in global poverty for the first time since the 1990s, with tens of millions falling back below the poverty line. Such a situation, I believe, calls for drastic action.

Extraordinary measures

In a recent working paper for the United Nations Development Programme, my co-author George Gray Molina and I argue that unconditional emergency assistance – what we call temporary basic income (TBI) – is an urgent, fair and feasible way of stopping people falling into poverty or further impoverishment as a result of the pandemic.

Looking at pre-crisis data that covers 97% of the developing world's population, we've estimated what the cost would be of providing TBI to all people currently either below the poverty line or vulnerable to falling under it. This equates to 2.78 billion people across the world's 132 developing countries.

We investigated three ways of delivering TBI:

♦ Top-ups on existing incomes among poor and near-poor people, up to a minimum level that is at least 70% above the poverty line in that region of the world.

♦ Lump sum transfers equivalent to half the income enjoyed by the typical citizen.

- ♦ Lump sum transfers that are uniform regardless of the country where people live. Under this system, the amount we simulated was US$5.50 (£4.30) a day per person, which is the typical level of the poverty line among upper middle-income countries.

Which option is best will depend on the situation. For instance, the first will only work in countries where registry systems have accurate information on what people earn. In countries where such systems are absent or weak, flat amounts according to general living standards (as in option two) or poverty lines (option three) might be better.

The total cost amounts to between US$200 billion and US$465 billion per month, depending on the policy choice. This is equivalent to between 0.27% and 0.63% of developing countries' combined monthly GDP.

It's a relatively moderate cost to cover such a profound shock and protect people from poverty. And providing TBI could have other positive effects as well: unconditional cash transfers can lead to people spending more money on their diet and can potentially improve health outcomes and school attendance. They can also protect people's assets and allow them to diversify their livelihoods.

Will we actually see this happen?

TBI isn't a radical idea. Forms of basic income are being rolled out under different names and with different funding levels around the world. Tuvalu has a fully fledged temporary universal basic income, and Spain has brought forward a minimum income scheme for low-earning households in response to the pandemic.

But our proposed scheme would be much larger – and would aim to reach as many excluded people as possible within the next six to 12 months. There are at least three obstacles to this.

The first one is administrative. Reaching eligible people who are currently invisible to official records and payment systems will require some work – they will need to be digitally registered before they can receive any assistance. Some people are beyond the traditional reach of the state because they lack formal documentation or live in informal settlements, which are more common in developing countries.

In these cases, alternative solutions – such as partnering with local social networks that have greater proximity to poor and vulnerable people – may be needed to find everyone eligible. The cost of adding each new person is not insignificant, but pales in comparison to the direct and indirect benefits of providing those people with TBI.

The second obstacle is obvious: funding. Given the temporary nature of the challenge, funding TBI by additional taxation could be politically difficult. Other ways of covering the costs are instead worth exploring.

For example, funds could be raised by repurposing nonessential spending, including wasteful expenditures and energy subsidies (which usually tend to benefit the better off). Alternatively, debt repayments could be paused for a period. Developing countries are expected to make debt payments of US$3.1 trillion this year. A comprehensive repayment freeze for 12 months, if possible, would fund 16 months of TBI under the top-up option, 12 months under option two and up to six months under option three. Also, as emergency cash transfers are often steered towards immediate essential consumption, part of the money will be recaptured by indirect taxation such as VAT and sales taxes, thus providing a degree of self-funding.

The third obstacle is trust. Governments will need to be trusted not to redirect whatever they raise towards other purposes, nor to allow temporary measures to last any longer than agreed. They will need broad (possibly cross-party) support to launch these schemes, and they will need to make sure that those that don't benefit from them still see the schemes as credible. These are all political challenges that need to be addressed on a country-by-country basis.

TBI schemes are not expected to reverse country-wide economic downturns, nor substitute for comprehensive social protection systems. They can, however, mitigate the worst immediate effects of a crisis that has been magnified by deep-rooted structural inequalities and injustices that haven't been decisively addressed in the past.

5 August 2020

Lord John Bird demands UK plan to prevent homelessness as eviction ban ends

The Big Issue founder spoke remotely to the House of Lords today and asked the Government to protect renters during the Covid-19 crisis.

By Hannah Westwate

Big Issue founder Lord John Bird today questioned housing minister Lord Greenhalgh on the Government's strategy to avoid a surge in homelessness when the current ban on evictions in England and Wales ends on August 23.

There are fears that 227,000 private renters who have fallen into arrears during the Covid-19 crisis could face homelessness if the Government does not move to protect them.

That's why Bird brought the question of homelessness to the House of Lords today, with just weeks to go until thousands could be put at risk.

'If people slip into poverty, then into homelessness, it is very difficult to bring them out of it,' he said.

Bird pointed to housing charity Shelter's urgent efforts to change the law and end evictions if caused by poverty driven by Covid-19 job losses and income cuts .

Labour's Baroness Blower stated that ultimately the Government should bring in rent controls and end no-fault evictions, but acknowledged both Shelter and Crisis's warnings – and said more must be done in the short-term.

She proposed 'emergency legal provisions to allow judges to prevent evictions where people have complied with reasonable and affordable repayments or are awaiting decisions on their benefit entitlement' as an immediate change which could avoid a homelessness disaster next month.

But Greenhalgh disagreed with the idea of rent controls, instead telling the peers that guidance has been given to landlords asking them not to evict tenants who might be sick or facing hardship during the crisis.

Earlier this year the Resolution Foundation reported that renters were 50 per cent more likely to have fallen behind on bills during lockdown as homeowners, while the majority of mortgage holiday applications have been accepted, little outside help had been made available to their tenants. Some renters said they were being forced to cut back on essentials like fresh food.

Liberal Democrat Baroness Grender mentioned the study and pointed out that in last week's financial statement homeowners were given a stamp duty tax cut worth £1bn 'while 20 million renters got nothing'.

Greenhalgh rejected the idea – instead drawing the Lords' attention to Government measures that 'strengthened the welfare safety net with a £6.5m boost' and increased Local Housing Allowance to cover the lowest 30 per cent of rent costs, plus £180m in discretionary housing payments for local authorities.

The housing minister again emphasised the steps the Government has already taken when crossbencher Lord Best asked if they had considered measures similar to Spain, where renters who fall into arrears due to Covid-19 are entitled to an interest-free Government loan to pay to landlords and remove the risk of eviction, with the loan to be repaid over a six year period.

A YouGov poll recently revealed that 174,000 private UK tenants have already been threatened with eviction by their landlord or letting agent ahead of the lifting of the ban,

The total number of people in arrears sits at 442,000, accounting for five per cent of the UK's renters, and double the number in the same period last year, thanks largely to the devastating economic impact of the pandemic.

Labour's Lord Kennedy of Southwark asked if Greenhalgh agreed a return to people sleeping on the streets would be 'tragic and unacceptable', that it 'must not be allowed to happen' and that it is up to the Government to ensure it does not.

In response the housing minister said it is the mission of the rough sleeping taskforce, led by Dame Louise Casey, to ensure the 15,000 rough sleepers brought into emergency accommodation during lockdown are moved on to settled accommodation as soon as possible.

Meanwhile Lord Goddard of Stockport reminded the minister of the importance of a 'multi-agency approach' to tackling homelessness for good, one that 'needs time and resources to get this right for people with complex needs' to prevent a return to the streets for thousands.

It aligns with the idea behind The Big Issue's Ride Out Recession Alliance, also introduced to the House of Lords by John Bird today – our new campaign to fight the imminent post-viral tsunami of poverty. Find out more in this week's magazine, available from your local vendor after they made their return to pitches last week.

13 July 2020

One in five people in Scotland now live in poverty – here's what's being done to tackle it

An article from The Conversation.

THE CONVERSATION

By John H McKendrick, Chair professor, Glasgow Caledonian University

Poverty is an opportunity, at least for politicians. The release of the latest annual estimates of how many people in Scotland are living in poverty – a disturbing 20% – provides yet another opportunity for politicians to blame other politicians for a problem. Holyrood blames Westminster, Westminster blames Holyrood – and those outside of government blame those who wield the power.

There are always people ready to embrace and celebrate poverty. Franciscan friars take a vow of poverty, and on occasion a media-hungry celebrity may choose a short period of living in poverty to make a point. And those reflecting on national sporting failings are prone to lament the lack of everyday poverty, which in the old days was the 'hunger' that drove our sporting heroes to achieve.

A national disgrace

But exceptions and distractions aside, poverty in the 21st century should be viewed as a national disgrace. It is pernicious – restricting opportunity, preventing people from reaching their potential and making life tougher and more fragile for those unlucky enough to encounter it. We should not forget that in these uncertain times of austerity, the UK is still one of the world's largest economies, with some projections suggesting that it will remain a top ten global economy until at least 2050.

What then are we to make of the latest estimate that one million people in Scotland are living in relative poverty – that is, after housing costs, they are left with a household income that is below 60% of the national median? Can the fifth annual increase in the number of people in Scotland who are living this way be viewed as anything other than a problem?

We could take an historical perspective and point to evidence that suggests that things are not as bad now as they were just before the turn of the millennium. The proportion of people in Scotland living in poverty has fluctuated at around 18-19% for the last decade, whereas it ranged between 23-34% in the 1990s. We might have just crept up over the one million mark according to the latest data, but we were always uncomfortably above one million at the end of the 20th century.

We could take a comparative perspective and point to evidence that suggests that things are not as bad in Scotland as they are in the rest of the UK. On the same day that the Scottish government published its figures, the latest round of UK estimates were published by the Department for Work

and Pensions. This shows that poverty is slightly lower in Scotland than in Wales, Northern Ireland and England as a whole – with only some parts of southern England outside London having comparable rates to Scotland.

But we still need a reality check. Better than bad is not good. A little bit less (in terms of numbers living in poverty) is nothing to celebrate. A staggering one-fifth of Scotland's population living below the poverty line is worth getting angry about.

The good news

The upside about the one million living in poverty in Scotland is that the country is actively doing something about it. Reducing poverty is not being left to the fanciful notion that a growing economy will cascade financial well-being throughout the land – or the equivalent myth that increasing poverty must be accepted as a fact of life when the economic climate is tough.

The Child Poverty (Scotland) Act received royal assent on December 18, 2017. Not so much an early Christmas present for Scotland's children, but more advance notice of one to come by 2030 when child poverty in Scotland is to be eradicated. Sound familiar? It should.

The UK had a similar goal until it was withdrawn in 2016 with the passing of the Welfare Reform and Work Act. When the UK government reneged on the Child Poverty Act 2010 with its goal of eradicating child poverty in the UK by 2020, Scotland dissented and set about introducing an equivalent goal for Scotland.

In advance of this Scottish Act being passed, a Poverty and Inequality Commission had already been established. It recently advised the Scottish government that making social security live up to its name, making work pay and reducing housing costs to the least well-off should be the key ingredients of a child poverty strategy. At the same time, it argued that steps to bolster the quality of life of children living with poverty should not be overlooked in the quest to reduce the numbers.

The Scottish government responded with Every Child, Every Chance, its first delivery plan for 2018-2022, working toward achieving the 2030 goal of eradicating child poverty in Scotland. New action on work and earnings, reducing the cost of living, social security and new forms of partnership working are all outlined in a comprehensive programme.

Poverty is never anything to celebrate. But at least good news can be found in those who want to take progressive and proactive steps to tackle it in Scotland.

5 April 2018

Key Facts

- Over the last decade, the average income before housing costs has grown less than over any other 10-year period since records began in 1961. (page 3)

- In 2018–19, only 12% of non-pensioners lived in households with no one in paid work, down by a third from 18% in 1994–95. (page 3)

- Despite temporary increases in benefits announced in response to the pandemic, the benefits system in 2020 provides less support to out-of-work households than in 2011. (page 3)

- Between 1 April 2019 and 31 March 2020, the Trussell Trust's food bank network distributed 1.9 million three-day emergency food supplies to people in crisis, an 18% increase on the previous year. (page 4)

- The top three reasons for referral to a food bank in the Trussell Trust network in 2019-20 were low income, benefit delays and benefit changes. (page 5)

- When unemployment benefit was first introduced in 1948 It was equivalent to 20 per cent of average weekly earnings. (page 7)

- Universal Credit Standard Allowance payments have fallen to just 12.5 per cent of average earnings today. (page 7)

- The Joseph Rowntree Foundation said that while paid employment reduces the risk of poverty, about 56% of people living in poverty in 2018 were in a household where at least one person had a job, compared with 39% 20 years ago. (page 11)

- 30% of single-parent families (in the UK) are living in poverty. (page 12)

- Approximately 14 million people are in poverty in the UK – more than one in five of the population, including 4 million children and 2 million pensioners. (page 12)

- Twenty years ago, 20% (2.4 million) of 20 to 34-year-olds lived with a parent or guardian. That proportion rose to 30% in 2018, affecting 3.9 million people. (page 12)

- The UK is the fifth largest economy in the world. (page 18)

- In 2018 the UN conducted an investigation into poverty in the UK. It found that:

  - 14 million people - a fifth of the UK population - live in poverty

  - Four million of these are more than 50% below the poverty line, and 1.5 million are destitute, unable to afford basic essentials

  - Child poverty is predicted to rise 7% between 2015 and 2022

  - Homelessness is up 60% since 2010

  - A 49% real terms reduction in funding for local governments since 2010. (page 18)

- According to the 2019 Focus Economics Consensus Forecast The Democratic Republic of Congo is the poorest country in the world. (page 21)

- World Bank data show that 35 percent of Mexico's population lives on less than $5.50 per day, compared to only 2 per cent of people in the United States. (page 24)

- Combined datasets from the US Bureau of Economic Analysis and the World Bank show that the poorest 20 per cent of US households have higher average consumption per person than the averages for all people in most nations of the OECD and Europe. (page 25)

- Department of Agriculture study found that US households receiving food stamps spend about 50 percent more on sweetened drinks, desserts, and candy than on fruits and vegetables. In comparison, households not receiving food stamps spend slightly more on fruits & vegetables than on sweets. (page 26)

- By 2015, according to the most recent data, 736 million people, or about 10% of the world's population, were living in extreme poverty, which the World Bank defines as living on the equivalent of $1.90 or less per day. That's down from 1.85 billion people in 1990. (page 28)

- In the past 40 years, China has taken more than 850 million citizens out of extreme poverty. (page 28)

- The majority of the 736 million people still living on less than $1.90 a day are in Sub-Saharan Africa. (page 28)

- Across the world, about one in three children – roughly 663 million – live in households that are multidimensionally poor, meaning they lack necessities as basic as nutrition or clean water. (page 29)

- Even in the world's richest countries, one in seven children still live in poverty. Today, one in four children in the European Union are at risk of falling into poverty. (page 29)

- Recent World Bank estimates show that according to current economic growth predictions – and if present levels of inequality remain unchanged – in 2030 about 6.5% of the global population will still be living in extreme poverty. (page 32)

- In 2018 the wealth of the world's billionaires grew by $2.5bn a day – or around 12%, whilst the combined wealth of the poorest half of humanity fell by 11%. (page 32)

- Globally, just four pence in every pound of tax revenue collected in 2015 came from taxes on wealth such as inheritance or property. (page 32)

- In 2018 it was estimated that one million people in Scotland were living in relative poverty – that is, after housing costs, they are left with a household income that is below 60% of the national median. (page 38)

Absolute poverty

Inability to meet even the most basic survival needs. This includes life necessities such as food, water, shelter, clothing and health care.

Affluence

Wealth; abundance of money or valuable resources.

Austerity

A political-economic policy to reduce government spending (and raise taxes) in order to try and reduce government budget deficits – during a period of weak economic growth or recession.

Benefits

Benefits and tax credits are payments from the government paid to people on low incomes, who need extra money to help them meet the costs of everyday living.

Child poverty

Child poverty refers to the state of children living in poverty and applies to children from poor families or orphans being raised with limited or, in some cases absent, state resources.

Developed country

Also known as a more developed country (MDC), a developed country has an advanced economy relative to other countries. In contrast with a developing coutry MDCs tend to have higher rates of literacy, life expectancy and gross domestic product, etc. Countries such as Germany and the United States are considered developed countries.

Developing country

Also known as a less-developed country (LDC), a developing country is a nation with a low quality of life and poor standard of living. The UN has come up with the Human Development Index which measures the development of a country by looking at rates of literacy, life expectancy, gross domestic product, etc. Countries such as Ethiopia and Afghanistan are considered developing countries

Fuel poverty

A household is said to be in fuel poverty if they spend more than 10% of their income on heating their home.

Minumum Income Standard (MIS)

MIS is a research method developed in the UK, and now applied in other countries, to identify what incomes different types of households require to reach a socially acceptable living standard.

Poverty

Poverty is a state or condition in which a person or community lacks the financial resources and essentials for a minimum standard of living.

Recession

A period during which economic activity has slowed, causing a reduction in Gross Domestic Product (GDP).

Relative poverty

A measure of income inequality: dependent on social context, the standard of resources which is seen as socially acceptable in comparison with others in society. This differs between countries and over time. An income-related example would be living on less than x% of the average UK income.

Sustainable Development Goals (SDGs)

17 goals set out by the United Nations to protect the planet and ensure that people around the world can live with equality and in a healthy environment by 2030. The goals cover social, economic and environmental sustainability. 'End poverty in all its forms everywhere' is the number one SDG.

Universal credit

Universal credit is a payment to help with living costs. It was introduced in the Welfare Reform Act in 2012 as a means of combining six benefits including housing benefit, working tax credits and jobseeker's allowance, within one scheme.

Activities

Brainstorming

- In small groups, discuss what you know about poverty:

  - What is the meaning of the word poverty?

  - What is relative poverty?

  - What is absolute poverty?

- In pairs, think about the causes of poverty in the UK today. What are the main reasons people can fall into poverty?

- Think about the ways poverty affects an individual or a community. Consider the following:

  - Educational consequences

  - Social consequences

  - Health consequences

- In small groups, create a mind-map of all the things that you need to survive. How many of these things are readily available to you at home?

Research

- Do some online research and share your findings on one of the follwing types of poverty:

  - Fuel poverty

  - Period poverty

- Do some research about food banks in your area. How many are there? When was the first one established and what can you find out about its usage?

- Using the webiste www.localgiving.org, research a local charity or community project in your area. Using this information, create a leaflet that presents the mission of your chosen organisation and explains to your classmates how they can get involved in charitable projects local to them.

- Conduct a survey asking your classmates, friends or family members about their perception of UK poverty and how they feel poverty affects them, if it all. Using the results from this survey draw conclusions about poverty and its impact in your area and detail the main concerns which you have discovered.

- Read the article *The poorest countries in the world* (page 20). Choose one of the 10 poorest countries listed and conduct some online reserach into that country. Look for news articles, statistics and organisations relating to the causes and consequences of poverty in that country.

Design

- Choose one of the articles from this book and create an illustration to accompany it.

- In small groups, imagine you are launching a new charity that fundraises to combat poverty in the UK. Design a logo, write a mission statement and create a leaflet to promote your charity's cause.

- Choose one of the articles in this book and create an infogram to show the information.

- In small groups design a poster promoting a charitable drive to collect donations for a foodbank or a homeless shelter. How do you encourage people to donate? Display the finished posters and as a class discuss which designs are the most persuasive and why.

Oral

- In pairs, discuss the definitions of :

  - Material deprivation

  - Destitution

- "Extreme poverty anywhere is a threat to human security everywhere." – Kofi Annan, Seventh Secretary-General of the United Nations. As a class, debate the meaning of this statement.

- Look at the various strategies for tackling poverty presented in Chapter 3 of this book. In small groups, discuss which proposed solutions you think would be the most effective.

- As a class, discuss how the following have impacted poverty in the UK:

  - Austerity

  - COVID -19

Reading/writing

- Imagine that you represent a UK charity and compose a selection of social media posts for Twitter, Facebook and Instagram. The posts should act as a series of hard-hitting messages which inform people about the effects of poverty in the UK. You may also post links to external websites, videos and photos which provide further information if you think this is helpful.

- Read the article *Rwanda invests in model villages to tackle poverty* (page 30). Write a list of the pros and cons of this development program. Overall, do you think it was a success?

- Write a 500 word diary entry from the perspective of a single parent who has suddenly had their benefit payment delayed. What difficulties would you immediately face? How does the worry and stress of it all affect you?

Acknowledgements

The publisher is grateful for permission to reproduce the material in this book. While every care has been taken to trace and acknowledge copyright, the publisher tenders its apology for any accidental infringement or where copyright has proved untraceable. The publisher would be pleased to come to a suitable arrangement in any such case with the rightful owner.

The material reproduced in ISSUES books is provided as an educational resource only. The views, opinions and information contained within reprinted material in ISSUES books do not necessarily represent those of Independence Educational Publishers and its employees.

Images

Cover image courtesy of iStock. All other images courtesy of Pixabay and Unsplash except for page 13 - image by MDI from www.shutterstock.com

Icons

Icons on pages 1 & 5 were made by Eucalyp, Freepik, icongeek26, monkik & Nikita Gorubev from www.flaticon.com.

Illustrations

Simon Kneebone: pages 10, 31 & 34. Angelo Madrid: pages 7, 16 & 33.

Additional acknowledgements

With thanks to the Independence team: Shelley Baldry, Danielle Lobban, Jackie Staines and Jan Sunderland.

Tracy Biram

Cambridge, September 2020